FINANCIAL DECISION MAKING

This book sheds light on financial decision making and lays down the major biases in human behavioral decision making, such as over-confidence, naive extrapolation, attention, and risk aversion, and how they lead investors and corporations to make considerable mistakes in investment.

It draws on a large body of literature, from psychology and social psychology to, most importantly, behavioral economics and behavioral finance. It also looks at the progress in behavioral finance research over recent decades and includes research outputs based on retail and institutional investors from the United States, China, and many other international financial markets.

The book focuses on China's financial reforms and economic transition and includes many cases from that country to highlight the importance of behavioral finance and investor education. It therefore provides much needed in-depth understanding of the Chinese capital market.

Ning Zhu is a Deputy Director at the National Institute of Financial Research and FanHai Professor of Finance at the PBC School of Finance, Tsinghua University, Professor of Finance at the Shanghai Advanced Institute of Finance, Faculty Fellow at the Yale University International Center for Finance, and Special Term Professor of Finance at the University of California, Davis, and at Guanghua School of Management at Beijing University. Prior to returning to Asia, he was a tenured Professor of Finance at the University of California. Professor Zhu is an expert on behavioral finance, investments, corporate finance, and the Asian financial markets. He has published numerous articles in leading journals in the finance, economics, management, and legal fields. In addition to his academic research, Professor Zhu helps asset management companies in a wide range of capacities.

FINANCIAL DECISION MAKING

Understanding Chinese Investment Behavior

Ning Zhu

Foreword by Robert J. Shiller

LONDON AND NEW YORK

First published 2017
by Routledge
2 Park Square, Milton Park, Abingdon, Oxon OX14 4RN

and by Routledge
711 Third Avenue, New York, NY 10017

Routledge is an imprint of the Taylor & Francis Group, an informa business

© 2017 Ning Zhu

The right of Ning Zhu to be identified as author of this work has been asserted by him in accordance with sections 77 and 78 of the Copyright, Designs and Patents Act 1988.

All rights reserved. No part of this book may be reprinted or reproduced or utilized in any form or by any electronic, mechanical, or other means, now known or hereafter invented, including photocopying and recording, or in any information storage or retrieval system, without permission in writing from the publishers.

Trademark notice: Product or corporate names may be trademarks or registered trademarks, and are used only for identification and explanation without intent to infringe.

British Library Cataloguing in Publication Data
A catalogue record for this book is available from the British Library

Library of Congress Cataloging in Publication Data
Names: Zhu, Ning, 1973– author.
Title: Financial decision making : understanding Chinese investment behavior / by Ning Zhu.
Description: Abingdon, Oxon ; New York, NY : Routledge, 2017. | Includes bibliographical references and index.
Identifiers: LCCN 2016053806| ISBN 9781138658165 (hardback) | ISBN 9781138658172 (pbk.) | ISBN 9781315619859 (ebook)
Subjects: LCSH: Investments – China – Decision making. | Finance – China – Psychological aspects.
Classification: LCC HG5782 .Z5763 2017 | DDC 332.601/9 – dc23
LC record available at https://lccn.loc.gov/2016053806

ISBN: 978-1-138-65816-5 (hbk)
ISBN: 978-1-138-65817-2 (pbk)
ISBN: 978-1-315-61985-9 (ebk)

Typeset in Bembo and Stone Sans
by Florence Production Ltd, Stoodleigh, Devon

CONTENTS

Foreword Robert J. Shiller		vii
1	Disappointing performance	1
2	Unsettled investors	13
3	Under-diversified portfolios	23
4	Mistimed timing and misguided stock picking	32
5	Disappointing mutual fund performance	39
6	Irrational mind	47
7	Behavioral biases and investment decision making	55
8	Difficult history	65
9	Learning by investing	75
10	Over-confident CEOs	80
11	Catering CEOs	86
12	Risk management! Risk management!	94
13	Regulation and government decision making: the behavioral biases of governments and regulators	102
14	How to reform	112
	Index	123

FOREWORD

Investing has aspects of a science, but it also has aspects of a game. Investing is like playing a game because one's ability to do it well involves the mastery of one's own impulses and an awareness of the presence of other investors with their impulses. One cannot invest well without a deep understanding of the relevant parts of psychology.

Most of us approach investing based on our basic instincts and intuitions. Most of us get very little instruction. That is how we approach most of life, since most of our education is general, and does not include a comprehensive list of instructions for living. I remember when our first child was born, and my wife and I brought the new baby back from the hospital. I wondered then: where is the set of instructions that comes with the baby? I was comparing our baby with any of the commercial products, like a television set, I have brought home, which always came with an instruction manual. The doctors told us very little, I thought, about what we should do to handle this amazing delicate creature that had just entered our lives.

Investing well is every bit as complicated a matter as raising a child. Psychology is important everywhere. It is a life-long activity, that must maintain a proper sense of importance, and, yes, it has aspects of a game and of competition to it. There can't be an instruction manual for investing like there is for a television set, because the game one must play with investing is so subtle. There cannot be a simple summary of things that need to be done: one must have a deep and general understanding of basics.

I have known Ning Zhu for many years, as he was a brilliant graduate student here at Yale. When he was at Yale a decade ago, we were going through a very active period in the development of behavioral finance, and Ning was a lively participant in this research. Since then, at the University of California at Davis and at Shanghai Advanced Institute of Finance he has been a leader in the field. I believe that he is eminently qualified to write an account of this revolution in finance.

Behavioral finance is a synthesis of activities not only of financial researchers but also of psychologists. The field is focused on helping people invest well. It represents some of the most practically useful information that everyone must know.

But the field is also just inherently interesting, as Ning shows in this book. It is fun to read. It is a field that gives some deep insights into all the human activities that comprise the economy. It tells us about naturally human efforts to deceive, but about naturally human efforts that produce great things for society.

The field of behavioral finance is just as relevant for Chinese investors as it is for investors in any country, for human nature is basically the same everywhere. I think actually that behavioral finance might be a little more important for an emerging country like China. The economic revolution that is going on in China is inherently psychological in its base and in its hopes for the future. A revolution as important as that in China since the Third Plenary Session of the 11th CPC Central Committee in 1978 opened up the Chinese economy cannot have been achieved without a kindling of the psychological spirits that drive inspired activities. Those spirits are ultimately reflected in financial markets, and sustained by enlightened financial structures. The best entrepreneurial spirit, which drives economic activities, needs to be cultivated, is delicate, and can easily get off track if psychological bases are not properly understood.

Ning's book covers a wide range of topics in behavioral finance, and serves as an introduction to financial theory more broadly. One learns here about the various kinds of financial instruments, with a perspective that helps us to understand their true significance. One learns about the history of major bubbles and crashes, and how human psychology has played a role. One learns about a life in business, and how financial incentives shape what we do. One learns about a life in government, and how people in government can view their activities and produce better laws and regulations. But most importantly, we learn how we can put together a view of the economic world that helps us to invest better, each one of us, towards a better future.

Robert J. Shiller
Sterling Professor of Economics and Professor of Finance
Yale University
New Haven, CT, USA

1
DISAPPOINTING PERFORMANCE

Invest to lose

On January 24, 2008, Société Générale, the largest financial institution in France, announced that the company had lost 4.9 billion euros (equivalent to 7.2 billion US dollars at the time), due to the fraudulent transactions of one of its employees. The news sent the company's share price plunging and its bonds were downgraded by most leading rating agencies. Thereafter, more details started to emerge as to what had caused such a large and prestigious financial institution to lose such a large sum of money so suddenly.

The rogue trader, Jérôme Kerviel, was a fairly junior employee in Société Générale's futures trading department. With his working experience in compliance, he managed to make up fraudulent trades to circumvent the bank's internal control and risk management rules and placed a huge number of unwarranted bets on Eurex index futures. At the peak of his speculation, the position that Société Générale held was 777 billion US dollars—much larger than the market capitalization of 526 billion in the same period.

Trading losses of this scale may be hard to believe, but they are far from rare. Dozens of trading scandals have resulted in companies losing billions of dollars. For instance, the US investment bank Morgan Stanley lost 8.6 billion dollars from its credit default swap (CDS) trading during the 2008 global financial crisis, setting the record for the largest single trading loss in the past decade. In addition, the US commodities trading company Amaranth Advisor lost 6.5 billion dollars from its bets on energy prices, which not only rocked the energy trading market but also cost the company its life.

A decade earlier, in September 1998, the once-lustrous hedge fund Long Term Capital Management, which was founded by some of Wall Street's star traders and several Nobel Prize-winning economists, lost over 5.8 billion dollars. These losses were so big and so devastating to the global financial system that the US Federal Reserve had to coordinate all of the leading investment banks to bail out the fund. Meanwhile, in Asia, the Japanese trading conglomerate Morimoto lost 3.4 billion dollars in its copper trading.[1]

The list goes on and on, and investors are often shocked that such specialized and supposedly sophisticated financial institutions can lose so much money. However, many investors—and especially retail investors—fail to realize how much they lose from their own trading, too. According to studies carried out between 1995 and 1999 in the Taiwan stock market, Taiwanese retail investors lost an average of 3.8 percent in their trading. That equates to a total loss of 940 billion New Taiwanese dollars, or about 34 billion US dollars, over those five years. Put differently, Taiwan's investors lost about 6.5 billion US dollars every year in the second half of the 1990s—not too different from the large losses that some financial institutions have suffered. Unlike the institutions, though, the retail investors' losses seem to be persistent and continuous. They continued to lose money every year, and suffered particularly large losses in the Southeast Asian financial crisis of 2007 and 2008.[2]

Such trading losses are quite sizable, given the scale of the Taiwanese economy as a whole. For instance, 6.5 billion dollars represents 2.2 percent of Taiwanese GDP, 33 percent of private consumption in transportation and media, 85 percent of household expenditure on apparel, and 170 percent of household expenditure on fuel and energy.

In contrast to the institutional investors' losses, which are difficult to trace to a single common source, retail investors' trading losses can be grouped into three major areas:

- 34 percent were due to government taxes, levies, and fees;
- 27 percent were due to commissions collected by brokerage firms; and
- 27 percent were due to investors' misguided stock picking decisions.

The remaining 12 percent were due to poor market timing decisions.

Aside from the fees and levies that retail investors paid to the government and brokerage firms, about one-third of all retail investors' losses were transferred to trading gains to their trading counterparties, namely institutions. To be more specific, retail investors' trading losses make up about 1.5 percent of the investment profits garnered by Taiwanese financial institutions. To some extent, then, retail investors—who normally earn far less than finance professionals—are providing generous charitable donations to investment professionals.

Such comprehensive trading records are available in only a limited number of countries, but it is still possible to discern the same pattern around the world: retail investors generally lose money, or at least perform worse than the market index. For example, Chinese retail investors' under-performance is worse than that of institutional/professional investors, and the Chinese A-shares market is close to ten times that of the Taiwanese market in terms of trading volume. Therefore, it

Disappointing performance 3

is quite likely to assume that Chinese retail investors lose ten times more than Taiwanese investors as a result of their trading activities.

The performance of retail investors

When asked about their investment performance, many retail investors do not really have a clear idea. Many of them will be able to remember a particular stock they bought recently and maybe that stock's performance. But they rarely know the performance of their whole portfolio. In some extreme cases, they will not even know which stocks they hold or the prices they paid for them.

Partly because retail investors do not see their investment performance in the context of their whole portfolios, and partly because they are not familiar with their investment performance, many of them are unjustifiably aggressive in their investment activity. As a result, their performance is generally lower than their respective market benchmarks.

In addition, retail investors have to pay large proportions of their investment proceeds to government and brokerage companies in the form of taxes, levies, and commissions. Furthermore, because retail investors do not have the same level of investment acumen and sophistication as professional investors, they generally lose some of their wealth to more sophisticated investors—without even realizing that they are suffering from a disadvantage.

If we were to form a huge investment portfolio by pooling the portfolios of all the world's retail investors, we could mimic their trading decisions by buying exactly the same number of the same stocks at the same time—and selling exactly the same number of the same stocks at the same time—as each retail investor makes a trade. The performance of such a portfolio would therefore reflect the performance of all retail investors. Based on such a methodology, researchers have found that US retail investors in the 1990s and Chinese retail investors in the 2000s both significantly under-performed the market index.[3]

Another way to evaluate the performance of retail investors is to assess their performance when they switch their holdings from one stock to another. Obviously, when an investor decides to sell one stock and buy another, she believes that the new stock will outperform the old stock. After all, every investor trades in order to make money, or to make more money. However, ten years of data from one large discount brokerage firm and a large retail brokerage firm in the U.S., and eight years of data from another large discount brokerage firm in China, reveal quite the opposite. The stocks that investors bought after selling their original portfolio holdings under-performed their original stock picks by a wide margin—3.5 percent per year. Surprisingly, then, retail investors tend to lose money when they trade, rather than make money.[4]

There is yet another way to assess retail investors' success, which is to track their buy-and-hold performance. With retail investors who hold their portfolios for a long time, we can simply compare their long-term performance with a market benchmark. According to research in the US and China, no more than 10 percent

4 Disappointing performance

of retail investors out-perform the benchmark. Of the others, about half perform about the same as the benchmark, while the remainder considerably under-perform the market index.[5]

Moreover, the net returns that retail investors are able to reap net of transaction costs (commissions, levies, stamps, and tariffs, and the price impact resulting from transactions) are considerably lower than their gross returns before transactional costs. Unfortunately, many retail investors believe that the more they trade, the more likely they will be able to make money. If such a logic were true, highly active retail traders would tend to reap high returns, and vice versa. However, researchers have found a strong and significant *negative* relationship between a retail investor's turnover (their total trading volume divided by the average size of their portfolio in a calendar year) and their net investment returns. That is, the more a retail investor trades, the lower their net returns tend to be. This phenomenon suggests that investors do not possess the necessary information to justify their frequent trading. Some of the "information" that prompts an investor to trade will be merely "noise" that does not provide much investment value. In addition, the negative relationship between frequent trading and net return suggests that transaction costs are so high that they erode the already unimpressive gross returns from high-volume trading.[6]

Evidence from the United States, Sweden, Finland, Israel, China, and Korea confirms the aforementioned findings that retail investors around the world all significantly under-perform their respective market benchmarks, both before and especially after transactional costs are taken into account.[7]

Many retail investors are surprised by—and often refuse to accept—such findings. A very common rebuttal is: "This cannot be true because I know for sure that I have made money from investing in the stock market this year." Investors in emerging markets, such as China, express considerable skepticism when advised to invest through delegated portfolio management channels, such as mutual funds or index funds. They argue that they want to pick their stocks themselves, rather than hand over control of their money to someone they cannot monitor. Others feel that they may be better at picking stocks than picking mutual funds or mutual fund managers, based on the reasoning that timely information on stocks is freely available, whereas information on mutual funds is often hard to find.

This phenomenon is directly related to many investors' subjective (mis)perception of their investment returns (a topic that we will discuss in greater detail later), but it is also linked to their lack of understanding of basic finance and investment. People tend to be very selective when digesting investment-related information and making investment decisions. On the one hand, many retail investors are under the impression that investment is easy and rewarding. Many of them are able to reel off lists of "friends" who have made fortunes from the stock market. And they generously share details of the good investments they have made and brag about how much money they have made themselves. On the other hand, they selectively forget about the stocks that have caused them to lose money. According to extensive research, investors are often unwilling to liquidate their losing stock picks. Instead, they retain them within their portfolios in the hope that they will at least break even eventually. This pattern of behavior leads many to forget about their losing stocks. And even if they are fully aware of their losses, few choose to discuss such disappointing investments in public. This selective communication of investment performance leads many retail investors to believe that investing is easy, even though most of them continue to under-perform the market index and other benchmarks.[8] Consequently, retail investors suffer from unjustified confidence in their investment abilities and investment performance, which in turn leads to them trading far more frequently than they should, especially in Asia. As mentioned earlier, the more frequently an investor trades, the worse her investment performance tends to be.

To make matters even worse, most retail investors often fail to realize that, for them to make money from investing in the stock market, they should expect performance that is not only commensurate with but much higher than the market index. Through their own often hasty and casual trades, retail investors can provide big favors to institutional investors, such as mutual funds. So, when mutual funds try to sell stock, they often find willing buyers among the ranks of retail investors. Similarly, when mutual funds wish to buy a particular stock, they often find that retail investors are willing to sell. Because retail investors are less sophisticated than the mutual funds, and because they often use market orders to expedite their transactions, they provide much needed liquidity to the funds, which enables the latter to reduce the impact of their trades and enhance their investment performance. In this regard, retail investors should be rewarded for helping the funds and should achieve investment performance that is significantly higher than the market benchmark. But they do not. As we have seen, retail investors significantly under-perform their respective market benchmarks in almost every stock market around the world.[9]

Many retail investors also neglect to include transaction costs in their calculations of their own performance. All retail investors have to pay (sometimes exorbitant) fees and taxes when trading stocks. Such fees and taxes result in much lower net returns. For example, US retail investors on average paid transaction fees of 0.7–0.8 percent of their principals during the 1990s. Transaction fees have dropped to 0.2–0.3 percent due to the introduction of online trading and discount brokerage services, but the cost is still significant if one takes into consideration that the average US retail investor will turn over her portfolio approximately 100 percent every year.

A similar pattern prevails in China. Even though Chinese investors on average face relatively low transaction costs of about 0.2–0.3 percent, they turn over their portfolios very frequently. With an average annual turnover rate of over 400 percent, transaction costs can easily eat away at any retail investor's gross returns, setting them back even further.[10]

In addition, retail investors normally use cash as a benchmark to evaluate their performance. Put differently, they tend to think of their gains and losses in the context of whether they have made money or lost money, yet ignore their investment opportunity cost, which is the performance of the market benchmark. For instance, if the market has risen by 10 percent in a year, and the investor has achieved a 5 percent of return on his own investment, he should realize that his performance is not as good as passively investing in the stock market. Relative to the overall market performance, the investor's stock has performed poorly, possibly reflecting the investor's own poor investment skills. Many retail investors fail to understand that their "success" has little to do with their own stock picking, and more to do with the fluctuations in the market benchmark. When they are unable to evaluate their performance relative to the benchmark, investors may develop false confidence in their investment ability and become even more speculative in their trading. If they cannot understand performance and benchmarks, or the true source of any investment returns, how can they make informed decisions and generate satisfactory returns?

Finally, most retail investors fail to consider risk when investing. They tend to focus on how much money they might make, while ignoring a basic principle of all finance and investment—the correlation between risk and return. Failing to understand risk leads many investors to misunderstand the source of their returns. An investor may generate impressive returns because he has invested in high-risk stocks (a.k.a. high beta stocks, which rise and fall more than the overall market index) and the overall market index has risen. Not understanding this mechanism, he may falsely believe that he has displayed superior investment ability and made an astute stock pick.

However, when the market starts to decline, the investor's stock will fall even more (simply because it is a high beta stock). Only then will the investor realize that the impressive returns he enjoyed were largely driven by the high volatility of his stock pick. Moreover, due to a psychological trait known as loss aversion, he will typically be reluctant to sell that stock now that it has started losing money. This is one reason why researchers have found that retail investors' portfolios frequently contain a large proportion of stocks that are well below their peak values. This reluctance to sell falling stocks means that the typical retail investor often relinquishes the gains he could have made due to the stock's earlier strong performance.

Professional investors' losses

It is not only ill-informed retail investors who lose money on the stock market. Professional asset managers—and even some legendary investors—have also made significant mistakes and incurred huge losses over the years.

Long Term Capital Management (LTCM), founded by a number of star Wall Street traders and two Nobel laureates, was a high-flying hedge fund in which everyone wanted to invest between 1995 and 1998. However, it suffered losses of over 5 billion dollars during the 1998 Southeast East Asian financial crisis and in the process almost destroyed the global financial system.[11] Similarly, George Soros, another investment legend, lost over 1.5 billion dollars during the stock market collapse of 1987, which cost him dearly in terms of both wealth and reputation.[12] A more recent example is John Paulson, who made over 20 billion dollars from accurately predicting the collapse of the US real estate and sub-prime securities market in 2008 but then lost over a billion of his fortune from the plummeting gold price in April 2013.[13]

In addition to hedge funds that actively invest in the secondary market, more secretive private equity companies have suffered similar losses from their investments. For instance, in 2007, Kohlberg Kravis Roberts & Co. (KKR) and the Texas Pacific Group (TPG) joined forces to make the Texas Energy Corp. private in a deal worth a total of 43.8 billion dollars, making it the largest privatization deal in US private equity investment history. To finance this blockbuster deal, the two companies ran up a total debt of 22.5 billion dollars. However, following a downturn in the energy sector, many commentators now believe that the deal has cost both companies billions of dollars.[14]

KKR was behind another blockbuster privatization in 2007—of electronic payment company First Data. However, because KKR took out a 2.3 billion dollar loan to fund the deal immediately before the collapse of the US credit market, investors can expect to suffer total losses of over a billion dollars when they finally exit.[15]

Behavioral patterns and biases may even influence and incur losses for long-term investors, such as pension funds. For instance, in a bid to achieve higher returns, the California Public Employees Retirement Services (CALPERS) drastically increased its investment in hedge funds and private equity companies right before the 2007–2008 global financial crisis. When the crisis hit, CALPERS' long-term pension investments suffered miserably.

Losses from corporate acquisition

Another major area of investment that often escapes public scrutiny is corporate acquisition. Mergers and acquisitions (M&As) are sometimes hailed as the most effective way to grow a company either within its existing sector or across business sectors. However, corporations that engage in M&As often incur heavy losses as a result.

For instance, during the internet bubble of the late 1990s and early 2000s, many companies suffered considerable losses as a direct result of their M&A activities. In 2000, Time Warner and American Online (AOL) forged the largest merger deal in US corporate history. Time Warner believed that merging with the high-tech AOL would help launch the company into the internet era. Unfortunately, due to the burst of the internet bubble shortly thereafter, and mishandling of the integration due to talent turnover and wasted investment, the two companies never managed to merge successfully. In the end, Time Warner was forced to spin off the legacy AOL business and wrote down billions of dollars as investment loss.[16]

Another famously catastrophic deal was Yahoo's acquisition of Broadcast.com. The latter was valued at about 5 billion dollars, and the buyout made Mark Cuban, the owner of NBA team the Dallas Mavericks as well as Broadcast.com, a billionaire almost overnight. One of the few people to remain cool-headed during the internet bubble, Cuban cashed in all the Yahoo shares he had earned from the deal just before the bubble burst. Yahoo's stock price never returned to its former heights, and Broadcast.com's was revalued at just 100–200 million dollars. It is worth mentioning here that many of Broadcast.com's employees refused to follow Cuban's example and sell the Yahoo shares they earned from the takeover when they had the chance. Consequently, they missed their one opportunity to cash out and watched their paper fortunes disappear.

Similar cases abound in corporate acquisition history. Terra, the Spanish communications company, paid 12.5 billion dollars for US network company Lycos. When Terra sold Lycos just four years later, it was able to recoup only 95 million dollars—a staggering investment loss of over 99 percent. Even giant companies, such as Microsoft and AT&T, have been unable to avoid similar mistakes. Microsoft acquired data analysis company aQuantitative for 6 billion dollars at the peak of the internet bubble, quickly realized that it would be unable to integrate aQuantitative's business within the corporation, and abandoned the entire acquisition two years after the deal had been struck.[17]

A more recent example is Hewlett-Packard's 2011 acquisition of the British data analysis company Autonomy for 8.8 billion dollars. Soon after the deal was concluded, HP learned that the majority of Autonomy's earnings had been fabricated. As a result, HP had to write down over 8 billion dollars just one year after it had completed the acquisition, 5 billion of which were linked directly to Autonomy's inflated earnings and accounting irregularities. The deal not only cost HP's shareholders dearly but also harmed the reputations of the bankers and accountants who had brokered the deal. It also resulted in several HP executives losing their jobs.[18]

The above examples present a compelling case that hedge funds, private equity firms, and leading public companies all suffer considerable losses due to various investment mistakes and oversights. Many of these errors are related to investor psychology and behavioral decision patterns. Therefore, it is not only retail investors who must pay close attention to risk and investor psychology; professional investors, corporations, and regulators need to be similarly vigilant.

Conspiracy theory?

Is it possible to say what causes disappointing investment performance? Many people in China would argue that the primary reason for their investment losses is that rival governments and Western financial institutions hold a hostile attitude towards their country and use sophisticated investment products and financial engineering techniques to profit from Chinese investors and destroy Chinese wealth.

Somewhat surprisingly, this conspiracy theory has gained considerable traction among Chinese investors and even government officials, who routinely blame foreigners for their investment debacles. However, such claims are not well founded. First and foremost, China is not the only country to suffer regular investment losses. At various stages of their development, retail investors and corporations in almost every country have suffered sometimes devastating losses.

Granted, China has experienced a couple of decades of very fast economic growth that has generated tremendous wealth along the way, and this may explain why Chinese investors are now so concerned with the recent setbacks they have suffered in their international investments. However, it is worth stressing that it is the United States, not China, that has witnessed the bankruptcy, nationalization, and bailout of some of its largest financial institutions as a result of the recent global financial crisis. Therefore, if any country should be blaming rival governments for its woes, shouldn't it be the US?

Apple Electronics' share price rose from 400 to 700 dollars per share before it dropped back down to 400 all within the twelve months of 2012. Many international investors made, then lost, a great deal of money as a result of this fluctuation. The following year, the price of gold increased from 1,300 to 1,900 dollars per ounce, before slipping back down to 1,300. No doubt the value of the Chinese foreign reserve has fluctuated considerably due to the United States' quantitative easing policy, but the US foreign reserve has suffered even greater volatility.

Similarly, when one focuses on the losses that Chinese companies have incurred as a result of their overseas acquisitions and investments, one should bear in mind that such losses are common throughout the global business arena. China is not the first—and will surely not be the last—country to learn the hard way about finance, investment, and investment psychology. One must understand that investor psychology and risk are responsible for many investment losses. Sometimes investments fail precisely because behavioral biases hinder investors from assessing and managing risk properly. To some extent, then, investors are their own worst enemies.

A second problem with the aforementioned conspiracy theory is the hostility it has generated. Many Chinese investors and executives who subscribe to it have become hostile to investment, finance, financial engineering, international financial markets, and even the global monetary system. Because of this hostility, some Chinese companies are not very open when engaging in international investment deals and remain suspicious of their international collaborators' intentions.

As the global financial markets become increasingly integrated, openness and collaboration have become indispensable features of almost every successful international financial transaction. Only through honest communication and collaboration can counterparties exploit mutually beneficial business opportunities and foster closer alliances. In this sense, a more open mentality is critical to the internationalization of the RMB and the further opening up of the Chinese domestic financial market. Blaming international counterparties and closing the door on the global market will not eliminate Chinese investment losses.

Finally, while those who subscribe to the conspiracy theory feel justified in pointing their fingers at foreigners, they are also, intentionally or otherwise, shirking their own responsibilities. Irrespective of how an investment loss has occurred, nobody has held the decision maker at gunpoint and forced him to make a decision. These are all mutually agreed, voluntary business transactions. Have the decision makers reflected on what they may have overlooked in terms of due diligence and risk management? Have they thought about how to avoid making similar mistakes in the future? Subscribers to the conspiracy theory probably do not address the problem from this angle.

Ultimately, this may be the main reason why so many Chinese investors are attracted by the conspiracy theory. It allows them to convince themselves that they are not responsible for their own investment losses. By reading this book, I hope you will be able to better understand your own decision making processes, and increase your knowledge of finance and risk. Thereafter, no matter who initiates a "conspiracy" or "attack" against your assets, you should always be able to make a sound trade-off between return and risk and accomplish a successful investment. If you are a retail investor, a money manager, a corporate executive, or a government official, you will improve your investment decision making and your investment performance as soon as you achieve a better understanding of both yourself and behavioral finance.

The investors' enemy

Why do investors lose money? In short, because the market is a risky place. Whenever new information arrives, one has to assess the risks and opportunities that accompany it. As John Maynard Keynes once said, "When my information changes, I alter my conclusions. What do you do, sir?"

Investors also respond to information, but in a far more excessive way than can be explained by the information itself. According to Professor Robert Shiller of Yale University—winner of the Nobel Prize for Economics in 2013—the US stock market has gone through several periods of excessive volatility compared to the volatility in prospective corporate earnings.[19] Before it crashed in the 1970s, it was trading at a valuation that was twice as high as the fundamentals warranted. At the other extreme, it traded at 30 percent *below* its fundamental value after the Wall Street Crash of 1929. More recently, it lost more than 30 percent of its value in 2008 before staging a drastic bounceback after the leaders of the G20 pledged to work together to salvage the global financial system.[20] Investors and scholars alike have been confused by the fact that the fundamentals and earning capacities of individual listed firms—though obviously impacted by the global financial crisis—have suffered far less extreme shocks than the stock market as a whole.

So, why have we experienced so many bubbles, bursts, and crises, especially over the past few decades? Why are investors unable to learn lessons from previous bubbles? Shiller and George Ackerlof argue that they keep making the same mistakes because of their "animal spirit"—their overly excited nature and irresponsible decision making.[21]

One primary purpose of this book is to help investors understand their own "animal spirit" and the limitations of their investment ability. If retail investors can better understand the limitations and biases in their own investment patterns, they will gain a new perspective on how to improve the management of their wealth and their portfolios.

Behavioral finance—the research area that intersects psychology and finance—has grown exponentially over recent decades, partly benefiting from a better understanding of how investors make real investment decisions and why they make errors. This book includes some cutting-edge behavioral finance research that should help investors better understand themselves, better understand investment and finance, and achieve better performance for their portfolios.

Many studies have pointed out that professional investors, such as mutual fund and hedge fund managers, as well as CEOs and CFOs of listed companies, are susceptible to precisely the same counterproductive behavioral patterns as retail investors (albeit possibly to a lesser extent). Therefore, this book devotes considerable attention to the behavioral patterns—and mistakes—of some of the most important investors in the corporate world. By doing so, it should enable such investors to overcome their behavioral biases and achieve better performance.

Finally, as the global financial system has become ever more integrated, global regulators are starting to shoulder ever more responsibility for its smooth development and stability. These regulators face challenges that are very similar to those that retail and professional investors encounter every day in the financial markets. Behavioral finance can certainly help them better understand themselves, better understand those they supervise, and better understand investment and finance in general. Therefore, I hope that this book will foster a new generation of leaders in financial practice and regulation, which will eventually result in a better financial system for the whole world to enjoy.

Notes

1 http://en.wikipedia.org/wiki/List_of_trading_losses.
2 Barber, B.M., Lee, Y., Liu, Y., and Odean, T. 1999. Just How Much Do Individual Investors Lose by Trading? *Review of Financial Studies*, 22(2): 609–632.
3 Seasholes, M.S. and Zhu, N. 2010. Individual Investors and Local Bias. *Journal of Finance*, 65(5): 1987–2010; Liao, L., Zhang, W., and Zhu, N. 2012. *The Performance of Chinese Retail Investors*. Working paper, Shanghai Advanced Institute of Finance.
4 Odean, T. 1999. Do Investors Trade too Much? *American Economic Review*, 89: 1279–1298.
5 Coval, J., Hirshleifer, D. and Shumway, T. 2005. *Can Individual Investors Beat the Market?* Working paper, Harvard University. Retrieved from https://papers.ssrn.com/sol3/papers.cfm?abstract-id=364000.
6 Odean, T. and Barber, B.M. 2000. Trading is Hazardous to Your Wealth: The Common Stock Investment Performance of Individual Investors. *Journal of Finance*, 45(2): 773–806.
7 Liao, L., Li, Z., Zhang, W., and Zhu, N. 2012. Does the Location of a Stock Exchange Matter? A Within-Country Analysis. *Pacific Basin Finance Journal*, 20(4): 561–582.
8 Odean, T. 1998. Are Investors Reluctant to Realize Their Losses? *Journal of Finance*, 53(5): 1775–1798; Dhar, R. and Zhu, N. 2006. Up Close and Personal: An Individual Level Analysis of the Disposition Effect. *Management Science*, 52(5): 726–740.

9 Liao, L., Zhang, W., and Zhu, N. 2012. *The Performance of Chinese Retail Investors*. Working paper, Shanghai Advanced Institute of Finance; http://faculty.haas.berkeley.edu/odean/Papers%20current%20versions/DoInvestors.pdf.
10 Odean, T. and Barber, B.M. 2000. Trading is Hazardous to Your Wealth: The Common Stock Investment Performance of Individual Investors. *Journal of Finance*, 45(2): 773–806.
11 Lowenstein, R. 2000. *When Genius Failed*. New York: Random House.
12 http://en.wikipedia.org/wiki/List_of_trading_losses.
13 https://en.wikipedia.org/wiki/Paulson_%26_Co.
14 http://online.wsj.com/article/SB10001424052748703883504576186962195399214.html; http://www.businessweek.com/news/2012-10-22/txu-teeters-as-kkr-et-al-dot-reap-528-million-fees.
15 http://blogs.wsj.com/deals/2011/05/27/biggest-private-equity-losers/; http://www.reuters.com/article/2013/04/30/us-firstdata-ceo-idUSBRE93T0WR20130430.
16 http://www.businessinsider.com/bad-acquisitions-2011-8?op=1.
17 http://images.businessweek.com/ss/07/10/1004_worst_mergers/index_01.htm.
18 http://www.nytimes.com/2012/12/01/business/hps-autonomy-blunder-might-be-one-for-the-record-books.html?pagewanted=all.
19 Shiller, R.J. 2000. *Irrational Exuberance*. Princeton, NJ: Princeton University Press.
20 Shiller, R.J. 1981. Do Stock Prices Move too Much to be Justified by Subsequent Changes in Dividends? *American Economic Review*, 71(3): 421–435.
21 Ackerlof, G.A. and Shiller, R.J. 2010. *Animal Spirits*. Princeton, NJ: Princeton University Press.

2
UNSETTLED INVESTORS

Transaction erodes performance

So why do retail investors trail the general market index? Many retail investors are surprised to hear that they are often their own worst enemies.

Based on a large sample of retail investors in the US and China, scholars have found that they often trade too much. For instance, in 2000, Terrance Odean from the University of California studied data from a large US brokerage company and found that US retail investors traded too often to be justified by rational motivations. He showed that the turnover ratio was about 80 percent per year in the US, and that those who traded more frequently obtained lower after-fee net investment returns.[1] (After the publication of a series of studies on investors' excessive trading, including Odean's, the turnover rate of US retail investors fell drastically.[2])

Somewhat shockingly, however, such a turnover ratio is quite modest when compared to the behavior of Chinese institutional investors.[3] Many Chinese mutual funds have turnover ratios that exceed 400 percent—that is, mutual fund managers shift their entire holding every quarter. But even this is dwarfed by the ratios of Chinese retail investors, who often report 500–600 percent turnover in an average year, and more than 800 percent in bull years, such as 2007.[4]

Such high turnover ratios can be partly explained by the under-diversified portfolios that are held by average investors. In the early 1990s, the average US investor held just four stocks in her portfolio, whereas the average Chinese investor held a mere three stocks in her portfolio in the early 2010s. The median number of stocks held by Chinese retail investors today is two, with about a third of all Chinese retail investors holding just one stock at any given point in time.

In China, it is widely believed that 70 percent of all retail investors suffer losses, 20 percent break even, and 10 percent make profits. Although this is difficult to prove with concrete statistics, it correlates quite closely with behavioral finance research which has found that between 5 and 10 percent of all retail investors manage to out-perform the market over the long term, whereas about two-thirds suffer persistent and significant under-performance compared to the market due to various investor behavioral biases.[5]

In any event, no matter whether we use turnover ratio or holding period as our criterion, there is a clear negative relationship between retail investors' trading frequency and investment returns in the Chinese A-shares market.[6] So, we must ask why this negative relationship exists. The answer lies in investors' purchase and sales transactions.

Over-confidence

First, those who trade more often than others do not necessarily know more about the stocks that they buy and sell. Based on data from the US and China, we find that investors who trade frequently do not achieve significantly higher returns than those who trade less.

One US study found that investors—and especially retail investors—are sometimes clueless about the securities that they trade. In the study there were two securities with similar tickers: MCI (a bond mutual fund—the Mass Mutual Corporate Investors Fund) and MCIC (a telecommunications company—the MCI Corporation). Even though these two securities had little in common in terms of their fundamentals, the researchers were surprised to find a very high correlation in the movement of their returns. That is, when there was good news about the MCI Corporation (Ticker MCIC), the price of the bond fund (Ticker MCI) rose too. The researchers concluded that many of the investors in the bond fund—most of whom were retail investors—probably confused it with the similarly named telecommunications company that they had intended to buy. In other words, the appearance of two similarly named companies on the stock market led many investors to buy stock in the wrong firm. Given that investors have trouble differentiating between a telecommunications company and a mutual fund, it is fair to assume that they probably make many other behavioral errors that result in highly active yet uninformed trading decisions.

The shorter the holding period, the worse retail investors' performance tends to be. Because retail investors often have unjustified over-confidence in their investment ability and/or information accuracy, their trading tends to be very active. They frequently realize their own mistakes soon after buying certain stocks, usually after incurring losses. As a result of such short-term investment setbacks, many then choose to liquidate the stocks that they purchased not too long ago, resulting in high transaction turnover. This initial over-confidence followed by panic selling among retail investors is believed to be largely responsible for the fact that net investment returns are significantly lower for those who trade frequently.

Transaction costs can be an important consideration, too. In the early 1990s, a one-way commission could be as high as 1.5–2 percent at some brokerage firms. Of course, this equated to 3–4 percent round-trip trading costs for retail investors.

Put differently, an investor would have to make at least 3 percent in any trade just to break even. Brad Barber and Terrance Odean have found that US retail investors who trade most frequently do indeed obtain the worst below-market, after-cost net returns.[7]

So, why do investors ignore transaction costs and trade so frequently that it diminishes their wealth? Once again, the explanation is over-confidence. Even though cross-cultural studies assert that Eastern cultures are more modest and introverted than those of the West, investors in China and other Asian countries display greater confidence in their own information accuracy and investment abilities than their Western counterparts.

One basic assumption is that rational investors should trade only if they expect to make a profit from the transaction or at least improve their current investment position. However, many investors in both the West and the East repeatedly engage in investment transactions that actually damage their investment performance. Many of them are surprised to learn that buying and selling stocks frequently harms their investment performance.

Scholars have studied investors who frequently sell an original stock (Stock A) from their portfolio and then purchase another stock later the same week (Stock B). Economic theory would suggest that, because all investors *should* be rational and non-satiated (prefer more rather than less, in economists' jargon), they must be convinced that Stock B will out-perform Stock A. However, financial researchers in China and the US have found that Stock B routinely performs 3–7 percentage points *worse* than Stock A over the next year. Put differently, investors do not really possess the advantageous information that they believe will make their fortune; and by investing on the basis of not so great information, they not only fail to profit from trades but also lose substantial amounts of money.[8]

Although good information should be the driving force behind all investors' trading decisions, researchers at Stanford University found that investors tended to trade for reasons other than good information even in the early days of capital market development. The study looked at British companies that were listed on the Dutch stock market. During the nineteenth century, the information relating to such companies could be conveyed only via regular boat services. Unsurprisingly, the companies' stock prices fluctuated dramatically whenever a boat arrived in the Netherlands. However, they fluctuated even more when no ship, and therefore no new information, turned up. Furthermore, when boats failed to arrive on schedule due to bad weather or mechanical breakdown, the stock prices still reacted substantially, as if some vital new piece of information had been delivered.[9] All of this indicates that investors have never traded on the basis of information alone.

Gender and investment performance

Men are generally thought to be more confident in their own abilities than women. Interestingly, researchers in the US and China have found that male investors are more speculative and trade more frequently than female investors. Partly as a result

16 Unsettled investors

of their contrasting levels of confidence, studies have found that men's investment performance is significantly worse than that of female investors. This pattern is particularly strong when the investors—male and female—are single.[10]

Consistent with the aforementioned study which asserted that investors incur losses when switching stocks within a single week, Barber and Odean found that male investors are more likely to switch their stocks in such a short time frame, and consequently suffer worse investment performance than women.[11]

Online trading and investment performance

Another piece of evidence relating to how over-confidence affects investors' trading decisions and investment performance can be found in the emergence of internet technology in the 1990s, when many US brokerage companies encouraged investors to switch from telephone to online trading. Needless to say, online trading has the advantages of speedier transactions and more user-friendly interfaces. What remains largely unknown, however, is whether this convenience helps investors achieve better investment performance.

Researchers studied a sample of over a thousand investors who decided to switch from telephone to online trading, and compared them with an equal number of investors of similar investment experience and portfolio size who did not switch to online trading. The purpose of the study was to track the first group's performance before and after they started trading online.

The findings were shocking. Although the investors in the first group had fared much better than the investors in the control sample when they had traded by

Figure 2.1

telephone (and indeed better than the market benchmark), their performance fell significantly after they switched to online trading. The apparent cause of this declining performance seemed to be the very reason that had attracted the investors to online trading in the first place: its convenience.[12]

The researchers found that the investors' trading turnover increased from about 60 percent over the previous 24 months (when they were telephone trading) to more than 100 percent as soon as they switched to online trading. Within a couple months of switching, however, their trading turnover typically fell back to about 80 percent. Although still significantly higher than their previous 60 percent turnover rate, the investors reduced their trading intensity largely because their performance had started to suffer significantly. If one takes incurred transaction costs into consideration, the switchers were not only unable to replicate their previous outstanding performance (when they beat the market) but indeed started to under-perform the market after switching to online trading. This under-performance then continued over the next three years of the study.

In contrast, investors in the second group (who stuck with telephone trading) maintained an average of 50 percent turnover throughout the study period and displayed no significant variation in their investment performance.

Consistent with investment decisions in the US, Chinese investors display very similar patterns in their investment performance depending on how they make their trades. We have found that investors' performance declines when they switch

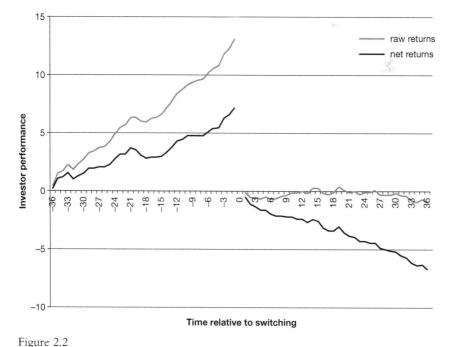

Figure 2.2

Source Barber, B.M. and Odean, T. 2002. Online Investors: Do the Slow Die First? *Review of Financial Studies*, 15(2): 455–488.

to an easier, more convenient, trading system. In particular, investors who trade over the phone achieve better investment performance than those who trade over the internet and those who use mobile phone apps. Therefore, it seems that speed may not always be the investor's friend, because convenience leads to over-confidence, excessive trading, and, ultimately, sub-par investment performance.

The illusion of control

A psychological term lies behind frequent stock transactions: the illusion of control. Psychologists have found that humans, when facing uncertain outcomes, have a tendency to confuse control of the process with control of the outcome. For example, in most casino games, such as roulette, players prefer to throw the ball themselves, rather than let the croupier do it for them. Although most people appreciate that the outcome does not really depend on who throws the ball, they still prefer to launch it themselves, because of the (false) sense of control over the process that this gives them.

Another example can be found in transportation. Most US residents prefer driving to flying for distances of between 250 and 400 miles. In order to understand this preference, the US Department of Transportation conducted a survey in which the drivers were asked why they did not want to fly.[13] Contrary to transportation safety data—which show that driving is eight or nine times more dangerous than flying—respondents cited safety as the primary reason why they preferred to drive. Some specifically cited "My safety is under my own control" as a primary reason for their choice, once again indicating that the illusion of control over the process affects people's judgment about the outcome.

Many retail investors, especially in China, are no different. They visit their stock broker's office regularly to exchange information and track the market's movement. Many of them, especially pensioners, start to view stock investment as their full-time job and diligently remain in the office during trading hours. Unfortunately for them, however, investment is such a complicated process and requires so much specialized skill and knowledge, that merely devoting more time to it does not guarantee outstanding performance. To make matters even worse, gaining increased control over the process often breeds over-confidence, which may induce more speculation and greater risk taking.

A counter-example to frequent trading can be found in the activities of Warren Buffett. He trades rarely, and only after careful consideration, and as a result he has generated outstanding returns. Rather than worrying about short-term volatility, Buffett has maintained a clear investing philosophy that has enabled him to devote more time to important thinking and rational decision making.

The disposition effect

Interestingly, though, retail investors' performance does not necessarily improve in line with their holding period. Indeed, some investors with very long holding periods (for instance, holding stock for more than two years) suffer very low investment returns.

This is a manifestation of another behavior bias that is widely documented in the Western financial markets—loss aversion. The same bias is probably responsible for a good deal of investor under-performance in the Chinese securities market, too. After an investor has suffered an initial (substantial) loss, they become averse to trading, and especially to selling their money-losing stocks, because of the so-called ostrich effect. Indeed, they refuse to make any investment decision, ignoring market news and fluctuations, and therefore miss out on potential opportunities to profit or at least reduce their losses.

In China, an evocative term is applied to selling stocks at a loss: "cutting meat." Irrespective of whether an investor acknowledges that his investment in a falling stock is due to his own stupidity or ignorance, if he were to sell that stock at, say, a 30 percent loss, the psychological impact would be significant and his confidence would take a hit. As a result, he is inclined to hold on to the stock, rather than cut his losses, in the misguided belief that the stock may eventually bounce back. By contrast, realizing the loss by cashing it in for a significant loss would be an admission of defeat.

This phenomenon is known as the "disposition effect" in behavioral finance as it reflects investors' disposition towards gains versus losses.[14] When it is pointed out to them, many investors quickly acknowledge that they are victims of the disposition effect because, on average, two-thirds of all Chinese investors' portfolios contain losing stocks. The reason for this is that investors are far more likely to sell winning stocks than losing stocks when prompted to choose which ones to sell. They continue to cling to the hope that their losing stocks may one day break even or even start to make a profit, so they are loath to sell them.

When behaving in this way, investors typically ignore two important facts. First, selling a losing stock does not prevent them from buying back the same stock a few days later. Second, there is time cost. Rather than holding on to their losing stocks, if the investors were to sell them and invest the money in securities with higher returns, they would probably make sufficient profits to cover their original losses.

Yet retail investors still display a strong tendency to hold on to their losing stocks and sell their winning stocks. For instance, in the United States, retail investors' tendency to sell their winning stocks is about 50 percent higher than their tendency to sell losing stocks. In China, the discrepancy is even greater, at around 75 percent. The loss aversion that motivates this behavioral pattern contradicts neo-classical economics' assumption of absolute rationality in investment decision making. Human beings care a great deal about both gains and losses, but the dissatisfaction generated by the latter often far outweighs the satisfaction generated by the former. Research using MRI scanners indicates that brain activity increases both before and after someone suffers a loss, suggesting that our strong aversion to losing has deep psychological roots.[15]

Professional traders at mutual fund companies and brokerage firms also suffer from loss aversion, albeit possibly to a lesser extent than retail investors. Researchers have found that mutual funds with recent manager turnover hold significantly smaller fractions of losing stocks in their portfolios, primarily because the new managers are not under the same psychological pressure as previous managers to see the losing stocks bounce back and break even.[16]

My conversations with seasoned traders at brokerage firms have confirmed this phenomenon. Inexperienced investors tend to hold on to their losing stocks, whereas seasoned traders are far more disciplined: they are prepared to cut their losses and liquidate their losing positions. Interestingly, even though some traders are very reluctant to sell their losing stocks and have to be ordered to do so on a particular day, they show little interest in buying back the stock the next day or later in the week. This is probably because their psychological attachment to the stock is severed at the very moment of sale, which indicates just how strong such psychological factors can be.

One legitimate reason for not wanting to sell a losing stock relates to tax. In the US, investors can deduct any investment losses from their taxable income at the end of each tax year. Therefore, if they sell at the right time, they may not only limit their investment losses but also reap considerable tax benefits. As a result, US investors are far more likely to sell losing stocks during December, when the tax-deduction benefits are most salient. The tax rules are different in China, so there is no comparable sell-off each December. Indeed, this probably contributes to Chinese investors' greater reluctance to sell losing stocks at any time of year.

Rational reasons to trade

First and foremost, information advantage should be an essential condition for every investment transaction. If an investor has the ability to foresee or analyze *positive* news about a company that will lead to an increase in that company's share price, then she should buy that company's stock. Similarly, she should sell stock in any company about which she receives accurate *negative* information. However, as we have seen in many examples of irrational investor behavior, investors are often far more confident than they should be in the accuracy of their information and/or their ability to process that information.

Another rational reason for trading is liquidity. After all, people invest in order to consume. An investor might need to sell her stock holdings to raise money for the deposit on a house or to send her children to college. The more diversified one's portfolio is, the less likely it is that one will be forced to sell one's stocks at fire-sale prices and suffer large losses.

A third legitimate reason to trade, at least in some countries, is taxation. As we have seen, investors in the United States and many other countries are allowed to deduct investment losses from their taxable income. Consequently, they tend to dispose of stocks before the filing deadline in order to take advantage of the tax breaks, even if this means selling at a loss.

Portfolio rebalancing is a fourth rational motivation for trading. Imagine that one has bought two stocks—in Company A and Company B—each of which is valued at 10 dollars per share, in the belief that both stocks will rise in the future. Company A does indeed increase in value—all the way to 100 dollars per share—but Company B falls to just 5 dollars per share. If the investor retains her original confidence in both stocks, the rational choice is to sell some of her shares in Company A and buy more in Company B, to rebalance for future share price fluctuations.

Finally, altering one's exposure to risk is a rational reason to trade. Investors at various stages of life have different investment objectives and risk preferences, especially with the shifting demographics in many countries. Typically, younger investors are willing to accept higher levels of risk in their pursuit of higher returns, while investors who are approaching retirement age tend to be more conservative, reducing their potential gains but also their exposure to risk. Finally, pensioners often devote large proportions of their portfolios to very low-risk bond investments because they provide guaranteed, if relatively modest, cash flow. Although equities, as an asset class, have historically out-performed bonds, with an annualized return difference of about 6 percent in the US throughout most of the twentieth century (11–12 percent for equities against 5–6 percent for bonds), most investors gradually reduce their stock holdings as they age, as they correctly view them as the more risky investment option.

Finally, let us summarize the main reasons behind rational trading:

- informational advantage;
- liquidity;
- taxation considerations;
- portfolio rebalancing; and
- adjustment of portfolio risk exposure.

These are all good reasons to trade. By contrast, stock tips from family members, friends, and so-called corporate insiders usually lead to losses rather than profits. So, if one trades for anything other than a rational reason, the likelihood is that the transaction will have a negative rather than a positive impact on one's investment returns and wealth.

Notes

1. Odean, T. and Barber, B.M. 2000. Trading is Hazardous to Your Wealth: The Common Stock Investment Performance of Individual Investors. *Journal of Finance*, 45(2): 773–806.
2. Federal Reserve of the United States. 2009. *Survey of Consumer Finance*. Retrieved from www.federalreserve.gov/econresdata/scf/scf_2009p.htm.
3. Liao, L. Zhang, W. and Zhu, N. 2012. *The Turnover and Performance of Chinese Stock Investors*. Working paper, Shanghai Advanced Institute of Finance.
4. Liao, L., Zhang, W., and Zhu, N. 2013. *The Turnover and Performance of Chinese Mutual Fund Investors*. Working paper, Shanghai Advanced Institute of Finance.

5 Coval, J., Hirshleifer, D. and Shumway, T. 2005. *Can Individual Investors Beat the Market?* Working paper, Harvard University. Retrieved from https://papers.ssrn.com/sol3/papers.cfm?abstract-id=364000.
6 Liao, L, Zhang, W., and Zhu, N. 2012. *The Turnover and Performance of Chinese Stock Investors.* Working paper, Shanghai Advanced Institute of Finance.
7 http://faculty.haas.berkeley.edu/odean/Papers%20current%20versions/Individual_Investor_Performance_Final.pdf.
8 Odean, T. 1999. Do Investors Trade too Much? *American Economic Review*, 89: 1279–1298.
9 Koudijs, P. 2011. The Boats that Did not Sail: News, Trading and Asset Price Volatility in a Natural Experiment. Unpublished paper, Stanford Graduate School of Business.
10 Liao, L., Zhang, W. and Zhu, N. 2012. *The Turnover and Performance of Chinese Stock Investors.* Working paper, Shanghai Advanced Institute of Finance.
11 Barber, B.M. and Odean, T. 2011. Boys Will be Boys: Gender, Overconfidence, and Common Stock Investment. *Quarterly Journal of Economics*, 116(1): 261–292.
12 Barber, B.M. and Odean, T. 2002. Online Investors: Do the Slow Die First? *Review of Financial Studies*, 15(2): 455–488.
13 www.independenttraveler.com/travel-tips/travelers-ed/how-safe-is-air-travel.
14 Odean T. 1998. Are Investors Reluctant to Realize Their Losses? *Journal of Finance*, 53(5): 1775–1798.
15 Dhar, R. and Zhu, N. 2006. Up Close and Personal: An Individual Level Analysis of the Disposition Effect. *Management Science*, 52(5): 726–740.
16 http://rfs.oxfordjournals.org/content/early/2010/10/13/rfs.hhq084.short.

3
UNDER-DIVERSIFIED PORTFOLIOS

Research based on data from a large US discount brokerage firm found that American retail investors are severely under-diversified.[1] About 30 percent of the sample held only one stock in their portfolio, while another 20 percent held only two. Put differently, roughly half of all investors in the sample group held no more than two stocks—a phenomenon that is consistent with the findings of the US Federal Reserve's Survey of Consumer Finance.

This pattern is even more pronounced in China, where about half of all retail investors hold only one stock at any given time, and more than two-thirds hold no more than two.[2]

Furthermore, in a comprehensive study of Taiwanese investors, we found that about a third hold only one stock. To make matters even worse in terms of portfolio diversification, if an investor happens to work for a listed company, then stock in that company is likely to make up 49 percent of their portfolio. In other words, an average investor devotes almost half of her investment capital to a single company—her own.[3]

Studies of Scandinavian investors have shown that, although mutual funds are probably the most convenient and economic means through which retail investors might diversify, they typically choose to invest more than half of their portfolio in individual stocks, and significantly less than half in mutual funds. Of course, it is not simply the number of stocks but the correlation between the various stocks' returns that ultimately determines a portfolio's risk profile. However, such a limited number of stock holdings certainly points to the fact that most retail investors have severely under-diversified portfolios.[4]

Why retail investors choose to hold severely under-diversified portfolios

There are several possible explanations for this phenomenon. First, retail investors are probably unaware of the importance of diversification, under-estimate its benefits, and/or over-estimate their own investment capabilities. To some extent, this is related to the over-confident behavioral bias that we discussed in the previous chapter. Whenever an investor decides to buy a stock, she usually believes that she knows all she needs to know about the company question, and therefore feels that she is making a great investment. Given such (over-)confidence in her own investment ability, why would she feel the need to diversify?

Unfortunately, this confidence often proves unfounded. Many investors soon face a troubling predicament regardless of whether the stock price subsequently rises or falls. When it rises, they fret about the best time to sell and pocket the profit. When it falls, the disposition effect comes into play (see Chapter 2) and complicates the investors' decision making process, hampering essential reassessment and adjustment. Moreover, in the latter case, once the number of stocks in a portfolio has increased because of the investor's unwillingness to sell at a loss, she may develop a false sense that she has achieved diversification—after all, she now holds more than the ill-advised one or two stocks. Unfortunately, though, all of her stocks are losing her money, *and* they are preventing her from implementing meaningful and worthwhile diversification.

Familiarity-induced under-diversification

Warren Buffett famously said that he only ever invests in what he understands. To understand something, one usually has to be at least familiar with it. As a result, many investment experts advise retail investors to buy stocks in firms they know reasonably well.

In general, it seems that most investors follow that advice. The Investment Company Institute (ICI) conducted a survey of US investors' familiarity with various types of investment and found that they were most familiar with the stocks of their own employers, followed by low-risk money market funds, US stock markets, US government bonds, other types of bond, stable-value mutual funds, global stock market, and balanced mutual funds. Out of a total of 5, familiar products scored about 3.5, whereas unfamiliar products scored about 2.[5]

However, this survey uncovered something else, too. When asked to rank the riskiness of the various investments, the investors clearly felt that those with which they were more familiar were safer than the others. In order, they believed that the global stock market was the most risky investment of all, followed by US stock markets, the stock of their own employer, balanced mutual funds, stable-value mutual funds, and US Treasury bonds. This risk assessment is paradoxical, though, because a more diversified portfolio (such as global stock market or domestic US stock market) will probably be much less risky than a portfolio containing just one stock (such as shares in one's own company). Nevertheless, familiarity with their own employers leads retail investors to believe that the most risky investment of all—in a single stock—is safer than holding a widely diversified portfolio. In other words, familiarity promotes misguided beliefs among investors.

Most people prefer certainty and seek to avoid ambiguity. When searching for investment opportunities, potential investors look for definitive answers and choices. Familiarity therefore leads to investment. If one is familiar with a particular product, service, geographical area, or brokerage firm, that familiarity will tend to outweigh any fear of the investment's risk. Similarly, there is wide evidence of significant home bias in international finance—the average investor is far more likely to invest in his own country's stock market, rather than buy shares abroad. However, there is little evidence that this brings advantages in terms of better information or superior performance for the investor. What is more certain is that most investors sacrifice considerable potential gains by focusing on their domestic markets and ignoring those in other countries.

My study of Taiwanese investors highlights how career familiarity influences investors' portfolio choices. On average, Taiwanese investors who work at listed companies invest 49 percent of their stock portfolio in those companies, while about 30 percent of all employees at listed companies hold only one stock—again, in their own company.[6] If access to advantageous information were the driving force behind such choices, one would expect corporate management's portfolios to contain even higher proportions of their own companies' stocks than those of the rank-and-file employees, who probably have much more limited access to such information. However, the exact opposite is the case: senior managers often hold very diverse portfolios, whereas the rank and file invest heavily in their own companies. Again, this provides support for the theory that retail investors favor their own companies' stocks because of simple familiarity, rather than informational advantage.

In addition, there is no evidence that investing in one's own company generates superior performance. Investors who invest heavily in their employer's stock do not achieve better performance than those who do not; and, similarly, employees who invest a high proportion of their portfolio in their employer's stock do not achieve better performance than those who diversify. On the other hand, because under-diversified portfolios are 20–30 percent riskier than a diversified portfolio, investors in under-diversified portfolios might expect 20–30 percent higher returns.

The preference for one's employer's stock manifests itself most vividly in the form of retirement pension investment in the United States. Research has shown that the pension funds of many large US listed companies (such as General Electric, Southwest Bell, Pfizer, and Exxon) invest more than 50 percent of their portfolio in a single stock—that of the listed company itself. Procter & Gamble heads the list, investing 93 percent of its employee pension fund in its own stock.[7]

Of course, such investment choices might be entirely justified and rational. Not only do loyal employees feel proud of—and indeed obligated to invest in—their own company stock, but also many listed companies provide enticing incentives (such as matching the employee's investment) to encourage their employees to invest in the business.[8] This may be done to reduce the threat of hostile takeover.[9]

Despite its appeal, though, under-diversification has several significant drawbacks.

A famous example of the perils of under-diversification is the case of Enron. Before it filed for bankruptcy, it was lauded as one of the greatest companies in the United States, partly because its stock had significantly out-performed the market over an extended period of time. In its prime, Enron's pension fund invested over 60 percent of its portfolio in the company's own stock. But when the firm started to flounder, its share price plummeted from over 100 dollars to just a couple of dollars. As a result, many Enron employees lost not only their jobs but also their pension plans and substantial personal investments, which were heavily biased towards the company's stock. Moreover, many of these people were then forced to leave Houston in order to find work, which led to a crash in the city's housing market. In other words, the demise of a single company wreaked havoc on its employees' wealth and wellbeing because of a reluctance to diversify. Other companies (such as Global Crossing and Kmart) have been similarly over-confident, with similarly disastrous results for their workforces.

Nearby stocks and stocks within the same sector

A Scandinavian study found that investors in Finland display a strong preference for investing in companies in their own sector.[10] For example, if an employee works for a technology company, his portfolio is likely to be tilted towards the technology sector. Similarly, an employee at an energy company is likely to tilt her portfolio towards rival companies within the energy sector. However, similar to our findings in Taiwan, investing in such familiar stocks did little to increase the investors' returns. Once again, then, we are led to the conclusion that focusing on familiar companies is more of a hindrance than a help when making investment decisions.

Another form of familiarity is developed through geographical proximity. The Finnish study found that investors living in the south of the country were more likely to invest in companies from that region, while investors living in the north were more likely to invest in those that were headquartered there.[11] My study of US investors discovered a similar pattern: those from the West Coast usually invest in companies with headquarters in California, while those on the East Coast put their faith and their money in companies from New York and New England. A related study found that investors in so-called baby Bell companies (local telecommunication service providers and breakups from AT&T) are likely to invest only in whichever company services their own area, even though all of these businesses are run along similar lines and have similar growth potential.[12]

Similar patterns are evident in China, too. Chinese investors not only choose companies with headquarters that are geographically close to their place of residence but also display a marked preference for whichever stock exchange is based in their home city. For instance, in our study, 17 percent of a sample group of investors from Shanghai had never traded a single stock that was listed on the Shenzhen Stock Exchange, while 19 percent of Shenzhen investors had never traded a single stock that was listed on the Shanghai Stock Exchange.[13] Interestingly, although it would cost only 10 RMB (2 US dollars) to open a separate brokerage account which would enable trades to be made on another exchange, about half of the investors in our sample had never traded any stocks on another major exchange because they had never bothered to open an account that would have allowed them to do so.[14] Such investors either have total confidence in the relatively small number of companies that are listed on their home cities' exchanges, or they are ignorant of the benefits of diversification.

All of these examples indicate that investors favor geographically proximate stocks, probably because of their familiarity with those stocks. But does such familiarity help those investors achieve better performance? Studies have shown that professional investors, such as mutual fund managers, can manage to leverage on their familiarity with a particular sector or with nearby companies and boost their performance by investing in that sector or those companies. One possibility is that geographical proximity facilitates fund managers' research of certain companies. Another plausible explanation is that geographical proximity allows the managers to establish informal social and information networks (such as school alumni associations or country clubs), which enable information diffusion. However, individual retail investors in the US and China do not seem to reap similar benefits.[15] Although they generally perform better when investing in geographically proximate companies rather than distant companies, their investment in these nearby companies does not help them achieve higher returns than the market benchmark, even before transaction costs and risk adjustment are taken into consideration.[16]

(Under-)diversification due to time limitations

One apparent reason why some investors choose to delegate their investments to professionals, such as mutual funds and hedge funds, while others choose to make their own investments relates to how much time they have at their disposal. Obviously, people with busy schedules have little time to devote to investment activities, so they may be forced to delegate their portfolio management to mutual fund managers.

Our research based on the US Federal Reserve's Survey of Consumer Finance and surveys in China confirms that investors who are married, have kids, earn higher-than-average salaries, and work in professional occupations are more likely to invest through mutual funds, and invest higher proportions of their portfolios through such funds. Therefore, the degree of diversification may not simply reflect an investor's sophistication and capability, but also their amount of free time.[17]

Limitations in diversification

Because individual investors normally hold no more than a few stocks in their portfolios, they tend to focus on the performance of each individual stock and fail to correlate the portfolio's overall performance. Moreover, even investors who trade frequently and hold a reasonably large number of stocks tend to have under-diversified portfolios because they make their trades over an extended period of time. If investors were to invest in a few different stock types, they may consider the correlation among those stocks. However, when they space out their trades and make one or two investments at a time, they may invest in stocks with similar risk and return profiles (such as all technology stocks or all high-growth stocks) without ever realizing that they are doing so. Such trading patterns inevitably lead to portfolio under-diversification.

Some individual retail investors are under the misguided impression that only large institutions need to diversify. Instead of diversifying by investing in index funds or mutual funds, they insist on investing on their own, despite ongoing disappointing returns. And even when retail investors understand that they should diversify, behavioral biases may prevent them from diversifying *effectively*.

First of all, many investors are under the false impression that simply increasing the number of stocks that are held in a portfolio is an effective means of diversifying risk. The benefits of diversification come primarily from the correlation of stock returns, not from the sheer number of stocks within a portfolio, so simply increasing the number of stocks without properly accounting for the correlation of their returns will not reduce risk. To give an extreme example, an investor who holds stocks in ten companies from the same sector may experience greater portfolio risk than another who buys stocks in just two companies from different sectors.

Our research in the US and China revealed that when the number of stocks held in an individual investor's portfolio increases from three to six (a 100 percent increase), or even to nine (a 200 percent increase), portfolio risk decreases by only 10 to 20 percent, rather than 30–50 percent, as one might expect. This is because retail investors tend to invest in stocks that are very similar to those they already hold. Even the small proportion of investors who hold more than 15 stocks in their portfolios (5 percent of our sample) expose themselves to significantly greater risk than a market portfolio, because they tend to invest in just one or two industries or sectors.[18]

The traditional rule of thumb in investment is that a portfolio containing 12 random stocks will be roughly equivalent to a market portfolio in terms of risk. However, given the increasing integration of the global economy and the world's financial markets, I would suggest that one would have to invest in 25 to 30 random stocks nowadays in order to achieve market portfolio risk level. Needless to say, few individual retail investors have the resources to hold that many stocks. Moreover, they will find it difficult to pick any stock randomly (i.e. without any personal bias or preference playing a role). Consequently, individual investors need to learn how to use mutual funds and index funds in order to diversify their portfolios effectively.

1/N heuristics in over-simplified diversification

Investors' diversification choices are heavily influenced by the number of options that they are offered. In a study focusing on US investors' pension fund investments, researchers found that, if the investors were offered more bond funds than stock funds, their portfolio choices tended to tilt towards bonds. In contrast, if they were offered more stock funds than bond funds, their portfolio choices tended to tilt towards stocks. Specifically, investors at the University of California who were offered four bond funds and one stock fund for their pension plans chose to invest about two-thirds in bond funds and about one-third in stock funds. In contrast, investors at Trans World Airlines (TWA) who were offered five stock funds and one bond fund around the same time allocated three-quarters of their portfolios to stocks and just one-quarter to bonds.

These are examples of so-called 1/N heuristics, when investors invest their capital on the basis of the number of options they are offered.[19] Put differently, when investors contemplate asset allocation and diversification, they do not seriously consider the economic fundamentals or return correlations. Instead, they think about the number of stocks or funds that they hold, rather than the correlation among those securities, and therefore make sub-optimal diversification decisions.

International diversification

So far, we have discussed diversification within a country's domestic market. However, as the Chinese financial market increasingly integrates with the rest of the world, Chinese investors are facing a new challenge: how to diversify their investments in a global context.

International finance research has revealed that investors tend to over-invest in stocks from their home country and under-invest in the rest of the global equities market. For example, the market capitalization of Argentina comprises about 0.1 percent of the global equities market. So, one might expect the average Argentine investor to invest just 0.1 percent of her portfolio in Argentina's domestic stock market and the remaining 99.9 percent in the rest of the global equities market. However, on average, Argentine investors invest 82 percent of their equity portfolios in the Argentine domestic stock market.[20]

And Argentina is not alone in following this pattern. The difference between what a country's investors actually invest in their domestic stock market and what they should invest in that market—according to international diversification—is almost always more than 50 percentage points. Specifically, the figure is between 50 and 60 percent for most European countries, including Austria, Belgium, Denmark, Italy, and Germany; 65 percent for the UK; 82 percent for the US; and more than 90 percent for many emerging markets. This indicates that investors in almost every country are severely under-diversified in the global equities market.

So, why do investors favor domestic stock so heavily? One apparent factor is capital control. In many markets, for example mainland China, investors are simply not allowed to invest overseas. But even investors who face no such constraints, such as those in Hong Kong, still prefer local securities rather than foreign securities. Another possible factor is transaction cost. Commissions for trading foreign stocks are often far higher than those incurred for trading domestic stocks. However, these two factors cannot fully explain the home bias phenomenon.

Investment opportunity is another potential factor. Investors in small markets are somewhat less home biased than those in larger markets, presumably because they have fewer domestic investment opportunities and are strongly attracted by the more enticing opportunities in foreign markets. In contrast, investors in markets such as the US and China feel little pressure to go abroad.

Familiarity and information advantage are other important motivations. Because many investors feel that they know little about foreign markets and much more about their domestic market, they choose to invest heavily at home and spurn the opportunities that are offered abroad.

Given that most Chinese investors would indeed face considerable informational disadvantages if they decided to invest abroad, how should they diversify? The short answer is through index funds that invest in either global or country markets. There are two widely accepted investment indices—the MSCI global equity index, compiled by MSCI, and the FTSE global index, compiled by the *Financial Times*. Both of these indices track the performance of the entire global market and cover about 90 percent of the total market capitalization of global stock markets. MSCI and FTSE also include regional and country indices, which track the performances of specific regions and countries.

An increasing number of Chinese mutual fund management companies have rolled out products that are linked to major country indices, such as the China Southern Fund S&P 500 LOF, the GuoTai NASDAQ 100, and the China Asset Management Company Nikkei 225. By investing passively in these index funds that track the performance of various global markets, Chinese investors can profit from international diversification without having to know anything about the fundamentals of the listed companies within those markets.

Notes

1 https://ideas.repec.org/p/ysm/somwrk/ysm454.html; http://rof.oxfordjournals.org/content/12/3/433.short.
2 http://rof.oxfordjournals.org/content/12/3/433.short; Liao, L., Zhang, W. and Zhu, N. 2012. *The Performance of Chinese Retail Investors.* Working paper, Shanghai Advanced Institute of Finance.
3 Lee, Y.T., Liu, Y.J., and Zhu, N. 2008. The Costs of Owning Employer Stocks: Lessons from Taiwan. *Journal of Financial and Quantitative Analysis,* 43(3): 717–740.
4 www.nber.org/papers/w12030; www.jstor.org/stable/10.1086/524204.
5 www.yumpu.com/en/document/view/44983872/2010-annual-report-to-members-pdf-investment-company-institute; https://ici.org/pdf/11_ici_annual.pdf.
6 Lee, Y.T., Liu, Y.J., and Zhu, N. 2008. The Costs of Owning Employer Stocks: Lessons from Taiwan. *Journal of Financial and Quantitative Analysis,* 43(3): 717–740.
7 Poterba, J.M. 2003. Employer Stock and 401(k) Plans. *American Economic Review,* 93(2): 398–404.

8 Cohen, L. 2009. Loyalty-Based Portfolio Choice. *Review of Financial Studies*, 22(3): 1213–1245.
9 Burrough, B. and Helyar, J. 2009. *Barbarians at the Gate*. New York: Harper.
10 Lee, Y.-T., Liu, Y.-J., and Zhu, N. 2008. The Cost of Owning Employer Stocks: Lessons from Taiwan. *Journal of Financial and Quantitative Analysis*, 43(3): 717–740.
11 Lee, Y.-T., Liu, Y.-J., and Zhu, N. 2008. The Cost of Owning Employer Stocks: Lessons from Taiwan. *Journal of Financial and Quantitative Analysis*, 43(3): 717–740.
12 Huberman, G. 2001. Familiarity Breeds Investment. *Review of Financial Studies*, 14(3): 659–680.
13 Liao, L., Li, Z., Zhang, W., and Zhu, N. 2012. Does the Location of Stock Exchange Matter? A Within-Country Analysis. *Pacific-Basin Finance Journal*, 20(4): 561–582.
14 Liao, L., Li, Z., Zhang, W., and Zhu, N, 2012. Does the Location of a Stock Exchange Matter? A Within-Country Analysis. *Pacific-Basin Finance Journal*, 20(4): 561–582.
15 Seasholes, M.S. and Zhu, N. 2010. Individual Investors and Local Bias. *Journal of Finance*, 65(5): 1987–2010.
16 Coval, J.D. and Moskowitz, T.J. 1999. Home Bias at Home: Local Equity Preference in Domestic Portfolios. *Journal of Finance*, 54(6): 2045–2073.
17 Zhu, N. 2008. Search Costs and Individual Choice between Direct and Delegated Portfolio Management. Working paper, University of California.
18 Liao, L., Zhang, W., and Zhu, N. 2012. *The Performance of Chinese Mutual Fund Investors*. Working paper, Shanghai Advanced Institute of Finance.
19 Thaler, R.H. and Benartzi, S. 2001. Naive Diversification Strategies in Defined Contribution Saving Plans. *American Economic Review*, 91(1): 79–98; Benartzi, S. and Thaler, R.H. 2007. Heuristics and Biases in Retirement Savings Behavior. *Journal of Economic Perspectives*, 21(3): 81–104.
20 Cooper, I.A. and Kaplanis, E. 2000. Partially Segmented International Capital Markets and International Capital Budgeting. *Journal of International Money and Finance*, 19(3): 309–329; Cooper, I. and Kaplanis, E. 1994. Home Bias in Equity Portfolios, Inflation Hedging, and International Capital Market Equilibrium. *Review of Financial Studies*, 7(1): 45–60.

4
MISTIMED TIMING AND MISGUIDED STOCK PICKING

Given most retail investors' under-diversified portfolios, they tend to trade actively in order to take advantage of their "confident" information on market timing and stock picking. However, our research suggests that investors who invest in mutual funds with a dollar average approach—meaning that they set aside a fixed amount of capital for investment on a regular basis—achieve the best performance of all mutual fund investors.[1] As a matter of fact, market timing seems to be much more difficult than most retail investors imagine it to be.

According to research carried out by Morning Star, investors made annual returns of 5.85 percent (excluding dividends) if they invested fully in the S&P 500 index during the past decade.[2] If a skillful or lucky investor had managed to enter the market at the lowest point every year (best timing), they would have made an annual return of 6.89 percent. Meanwhile, an investor who entered the market at the highest point every year (worst timing) would have made 5.02 percent. In other words, investors with perfect timing might expect annual returns that are almost 2 percentage points (or 40 percent) higher than those achieved by investors with terrible timing.

The same report also found that, if an investor invested fully in the S&P 500 over the previous 20 years, her return on investment would be 7.81 percent. However, if she missed the market's 10 best-performing days, her return would drop to 4.14 percent, and if she missed the 20 best-performing days, her return would drop to just 1.70 percent—much lower than the fully invested scenario. Once again, this finding confirms that timing is crucial to achieving good returns. But it is not easy.

In terms of calendar effect, September and October tend to be the riskiest months. The stock market crash of 1987, the Southeast Asian financial crisis of 1998, the terrorist attack on the World Trade Center of 2001, and the bankruptcy of Lehman Brothers in 2008 all took place during those months. To some extent, this explains why there is a "Halloween effect" in the US investment market—investing in October and liquidating before the following summer has tended to be a relatively safe and profitable strategy. On average, December reports the worst performance and January the best in the US, partly due to the December tax filing motivation. Similarly, in China, there is a well-documented "Spring Festival" effect, with a bullish run often occurring around the time of the Chinese new year in January or February.

Therefore, investors clearly need to be diversified not only in terms of their portfolios but also in terms of their market timing. They must understand that market timing is difficult—maybe even more difficult than choosing the best stock. Consequently, they should diversify in terms of entry points into and exit points out of the market, rather than jumping in and out all at once.

Unfortunately, most retail investors do the latter. Just as they display over-confidence when picking particular stocks, they are over-confident in their ability when it comes to market timing. Trend chasing is a very common retail investor trait. After the price of gold increased from 300 dollars per ounce in 2002 to 1,900 dollars per ounce in 2012, many people predicted it would go on to exceed 3,000 dollars per ounce over the next few years. However, it plummeted by about 30 percent over the next few months. Similarly, the share price of Apple Computers jumped from 400 dollars per share in early 2012 to 700 dollars by the summer, with many investors predicting it would keep on rising and buying the stock at the higher price as a result. In fact, it had fallen back to about 400 dollars just a few months later, leaving many investors stupefied and out of pocket.

There is similar over-confidence in the Chinese housing market. Because house prices have climbed steadily over the past 20 years, many Chinese households now presume that they will keep rising for ever. However, there is no guarantee that past returns will lead to future returns. Nobel laureate Daniel Kahneman terms this pattern of behavior "representative bias." This means that human beings tend to over-value salient, recent, and easy-to-process information but under-value probabilistic evidence based on large samples.

Each stock market has its own rules and rhythms. For example, the US market returned an average of about 11 percent between 1926 and 1996, while the Chinese market returned an average of about 18 percent in the two decades after its establishment. The crucial point for our discussion is that these are *average* returns over relatively long periods of time, so the returns would have been higher than average in some years, and lower than average in others. For example, the US stock market enjoyed one of its best runs in the 1990s, when some professional investors started warning retail investors to under-weight US stocks, because it was unlikely that the market's performance would continue to deviate from its average for much longer. Unfortunately, many investors turned a deaf ear to this advice. After the internet bubble, they became increasingly bullish about what would happen next, and over-weighed risky assets such as growth stocks and private equity funds.

As it turned out, the S&P 500 index barely grew during the 2000s, starting at about 10,000 points and ending at about 10,000 points, partly due to the

2008 global financial crisis. To some extent, this disappointing performance may be explained by the rule of regression towards the mean—the outstanding performance of the 1990s was balanced by the poor performance of the subsequent decade.

In this context, investors' capital flow often serves as a reliable negative predictor of the future direction of market movement. In both US and Chinese stock markets, periods of exceptionally high inflow from retail investors (1998 in the US and 2008 in China) have turned out to be harbingers of a market crash. In contrast, the market started to rise just after retail investors decided to leave it en masse (e.g. 2011–2012 in the US and late 2008 in China).[3] That is, retail investors pour money into the stock market at the very moment when their future returns are least promising, and vice versa.

Warren Buffett once explained the secret to his success as follows: "I become scared when others get greedy, and greedy when others get scared." By contrast, most retail investors follow the herd: they get greedy when others get greedy, and scared when others get scared.

Herding and delayed reaction

Many animals move in herds, and many humans do the same.[4] Specifically, retail investors often base their investment decisions on what they have heard other retail investors are doing.

There are some merits to this approach, at least in the short term. Because retail investors follow each other's decisions, early enterers may make short-term profits, partly because those who follow their lead and buy the same stock push up the share price. However, these short-term gains are rarely supported by superior fundamentals. Rather, they are driven solely by a retail investor frenzy. As a result, the stock will not maintain its high level for very long before falling back to (or below) its original price.

Typically, institutions try to obtain and trade upon information as soon as it becomes available. However, because stock prices start to move in the direction in which the information points as soon as more people start to trade on the basis of it, the value of the information is short lived and decreases over time. This explains why the institutions react to their own information immediately but disregard any that they know others have received first.

In contrast, our research in the United States and China reveals a very different pattern among retail investors: they all react to the same piece of information in the same way (buying or selling a certain stock on the basis of the information), but in a *gradual* fashion. Partly this is because individual investors do not pay attention to their investments all the time. Also, they tend to obtain information from chatting with friends and TV reports, so there is bound to be a time lag between the information entering the public domain and the individual investor hearing it. Hence, many retail investors trade on the basis of information that is days, weeks, or even months old.[5] Needless to say, such old information never helps these investors achieve outstanding investment performance. Indeed, it often causes them to buy a stock just when better-informed (or earlier-informed) investors know that the share price has reached its peak.

Misguided stock picking

Individual retail investors tend to favor stocks that have just reached new highs or new lows, stocks that are discussed in the popular media, and stocks with unusually large trading volumes. In other words, their decisions are based on which companies have attracted their attention, not on accurate information about the fundamentals of those companies.[6]

It is also worth mentioning that investors' buying and selling decisions are often very different processes. Purchases often involve choosing among a large number of options. For instance, more than 10,000 stocks are listed on the various US stock markets and more than 3,000 are listed in China. An individual investor is therefore highly unlikely to have the time or the inclination to sift through all of the information pertaining to all of those stocks. Instead, she will probably choose a stock that has come to her attention in some way, which explains why listed companies devote so much time and money to attracting new investors. After all, investors only ever tend to buy what they know.[7] Researchers have found that individual investors in the US are very responsive to stock recommendations that they receive through newsletters, buying plenty of shares in whichever companies featured in the latest issues. In contrast, investment institutions ignore the newsletters, as they are well aware that the information they contain is already in the public domain and therefore of little value.[8]

A related study found that, in the 1990s, when print media was still popular, investors' responses to stock-related information were heavily dependent on when that piece of information appeared in their local newspaper. The same piece of news might be published on different dates in different locations, and investment in the company in question would be closely linked to when the article appeared in each location. Once again, this confirms that investors trade on the basis of what they see with their own eyes.[9]

A prime example of this phenomenon concerns trading in EntreMed, a listed pharmaceutical company. On Monday, May 4, 1998, EntreMed's share price jumped by more than 50 percent, with a trading volume several times higher than the company's average over the previous few months. The explanation was simple: the weekend edition of the *New York Times* had featured a very positive article on the company's new cancer drug, so investors had rushed to buy the stock as soon as the market opened.[10] However, the important point for our discussion is that very similar articles had appeared in the *Wall Street Journal* and the academic journal *Science* several months earlier, but they had caused barely a ripple in trading in EntreMed. The only logical conclusion is that far more retail investors saw the *New York Times* article and then reacted to the "news" long after it had actually entered the public domain.

Of course, listed companies are well aware that potential investors respond in this way, so they often try to attract attention in order to manipulate the investors' judgment and decision making. For instance, companies with better-than-expected earnings often announce their profits on dates when few other companies are making announcements. Similarly, companies that have fallen short of market expectations frequently time their announcements to coincide with those of several other companies in the hope that any criticism will be diluted.[11]

Familiarity-based stock picking

Familiarity is another motivating factor that influences investors' decisions. We have already seen that investors tend to buy stocks only in companies that they know relatively well. For instance, geographical proximity is important. In our home cities we interact with friends, read local newspapers, and enjoy the services that are provided by local companies. Such familiarity not only increases our awareness of local companies but often encourages us to invest in them.[12] Potential investors are also likely to invest in line with their own careers. The theory goes that investing in one's own industry or a certain type of technology with which one is familiar will inevitably lead to higher returns than investing in a sector about which one knows little or nothing.

Unfortunately, neither geographical proximity nor industry affiliation seems to help retail investors achieve better-than-market performance. (However, it should be noted that such "familiar" investments do out-perform other stocks in retail investors' portfolios, which tend to generate even lower returns.)

Corporate names

Neo-classical finance theory asserts that stock investment decisions should be based solely on dividend-related fundamental information. However, there is strong evidence to suggest that company name, company ticker, and name/ticker complexity all have a bearing on investors' choices. For instance, during the internet bubble, many listed companies simply changed their names so that they ended in ".com." Interestingly, investors seemed to welcome these name changes—on average the company's share price would jump by more than 70 percent in the course of the next month, even though no substantive change had been made to the business itself. Similarly, in the United States in the 1950s, many companies changed their names so they ended in "-tronics" in order to benefit from the electronics fever that was gripping the nation.[13] Clearly, then, a company's name can have a significant impact on investor awareness and recognition, which in turn can influence their decision making. Mutual funds may also change their names in order to attract investors' attention and capital inflow.[14]

In Asia, some numbers (such as 8 and 6) are believed to be auspicious, whereas others (such as 4) are viewed as ominous, so, unsurprisingly, far more company tickers feature 8 or 6 than other numbers (particularly 4). Of course, everyone understands that the ticker number says nothing about any company's fundamentals, but such businesses appreciate that it can have a profound psychological impact on potential investors' decisions.

Furthermore, in my research I have found that Chinese investors favor companies with three-character tickers to those with four-character tickers, presumably because the former are easier to process and understand. Also, tickers with "easier" characters (those with fewer strokes and/or those that appear frequently in daily life) attract more investors in the immediate aftermath of an initial public offering, enjoy a broader investor base and more liquid trading in the secondary market, and tend to have a higher valuation. Again, then, factors that bear no relation to company fundamentals seem to exert considerable influence over investors' decisions.[15]

Summary

In sum, individuals' market timing decisions and stock picking decisions are often sub-optimal and heavily influenced by psychological factors and behavioral biases. Performance is therefore open to significant improvement once investors become aware of errors they make.

Notes

1 Liao, L., Zhang, W., and Zhu, N. 2012. *The Performance of Chinese Mutual Fund Investors*. Working paper, Shanghai Advanced Institute of Finance.
2 www.morningstar.com/products/institutional/PDF/Nov12_Release.pdf.
3 Dichev, I.D. 2007. What Are Stock Investors' Actual Historical Returns? Evidence from Dollar-Weighted Returns. *American Economic Review*, 97(1): 386–401.
4 Zhu, N. 2003. *The Herding of Individual Investors*. Working paper, Yale University.
5 Barber, B.M., Odean, T., and Zhu, N. 2009. Systematic Noise. *Journal of Financial Markets*, 12(4): 547–569.
6 Barber, B.M. and Odean, T. 2008. All that Glitters: The Effect of Attention and News on the Buying Behavior of Individual and Institutional Investors. *Review of Financial Studies*, 21(2): 785–818.
7 Zhu, N. 2003. *The Local Bias of Individual Investors*. Working paper, Yale University.
8 Kumar, A. and Pons, V. 2002. *Behavior and Performance of Investment Newsletters Analysts*. Working paper, Yale School of Management.
9 http://citeseerx.ist.psu.edu/viewdoc/download?doi=10.1.1.394.7983&rep=rep1&type=pdf.
10 Huberman, G. and Regev, T. 2001. Contagious Speculation and a Cure for Cancer: A Nonevent that Made Stock Prices Soar. *Journal of Finance*, 56(1): 387–396.
11 Hirshleifer, D. and Teoh, S.H. 2003. Limited Attention, Information Disclosure, and Financial Reporting. *Journal of Accounting and Economics*, 36(1): 337–386; Hirshleifer, D., Lim, S.S., and Teoh, S.H. 2009. Driven to Distraction: Extraneous Events and Underreaction to Earnings News. *Journal of Finance*, 64(5): 2289–2325.
12 Seasholes, M.S. and Zhu, N. 2010. Individual Investors and Local Bias. *Journal of Finance*, 65(5): 1987–2010.
13 Cooper, M.J., Dimitrov, O., and Rau, P.R. 2001. A Rose.com by Any Other Name. *Journal of Finance*, 56(6): 2371–2388.

14 Cooper, M.J., Gulen, H., and Rau, P.R. 2005. Changing Names with Style: Mutual Fund Name Changes and Their Effects on Fund Flows. *Journal of Finance*, 60(6): 2825–2858.
15 Fang, C. and Zhu, N. 2016. *Name Complexity and Portfolio Choice*. Working paper, Shanghai Advanced Institute of Finance.

5
DISAPPOINTING MUTUAL FUND PERFORMANCE

As more and more individual investors realize that they are not great investors in the stock market, more and more of them are switching some of their money into mutual funds. However, research in China has revealed that investors face similar challenges in their mutual fund investment decisions as when they go it alone.

Excessive trading in mutual fund investment

Unlike foreign mutual fund investors, Chinese mutual fund investors trade frequently—as if they are trading individual stocks. The average turnover rate for Chinese mutual fund investors has been about 120 percent since the year 2000, with an average holding period of nine to ten months. This turnover rate is considerably higher than the average for US investors' stock investments in the 1990s.[1]

The problem with such high turnover rates is that mutual fund investment involves far higher transaction costs than the trading of individual stocks. Mutual fund investors have to pay not only management fees and marketing-related fees but also fees for transacting mutual fund shares. In order to increase their investment cash flow, mutual funds typically impose front-end *and* rear-end load to deter investors from buying and selling mutual fund shares too frequently.[2]

Chinese mutual fund management companies charge significantly higher fees than their foreign counterparts. The average management fees are 1.23 percent (or 1.46 percent if index funds are excluded) for Chinese equity mutual funds, 0.77 percent for Chinese bond funds, and about 0.7 percent for index funds. In contrast, the international average is about 1 percent for equity mutual funds, 0.3–0.4 percent for bond funds, and 0.1–0.2 percent for index funds. In other words, Chinese funds often charge 50 or even 100 percent more than the international average. It could be argued that it is reasonable for actively managed Chinese funds to charge higher fees because of the complex nature of the Chinese domestic market, but it is difficult to understand why passively managed index funds charge higher fees than their international counterparts.

In addition to their management fees, investment companies charge a custodian fee (0.21 percent on average), front-end load (1.49 percent on average), and rear-end load (0.51 percent on average). As most Chinese mutual fund investors trade frequently, these loads can significantly erode the returns on their investments. Indeed, all individual investors should calculate and acknowledge how much wealth they are forsaking by trading frequently in mutual funds. Based on the average turnover ratio of 120 percent, the average Chinese equity mutual fund investor incurs about 3.5–4 percent annualized management fees of about 4.07 percent (1.5% management fee + 0.21% custodian fee + 1.2 * (1.44% front load + 0.51% rear load) * 2.4 (average turnover for Chinese mutual fund investors)). This is about 80 percent more than the international average, and more than twice as much as a typical US mutual fund would levy. Therefore, Chinese investors have to understand that frequent trading is hazardous to their wealth in mutual fund investment, just as in individual stock investment.

The legend of William Miller

William Miller, who managed the Legg Mason fund, is a legendary figure in American investment. He delivered some amazing returns between 1991 and 2005, exceeding the S&P 500 index every single year, even after his management fees were deducted. Put differently, any investor putting money into Miller's mutual fund could rest easy that she was out-performing the market over the course of fifteen profitable years.

If we analogize defeating the market to flipping a coin, the chance of a mutual fund manager beating the market for fifteen years in a row is equivalent to flipping fifteen consecutive heads and no tails—a chance of 1 in 32,768. However, because one should always take management fees into account before assessing the returns from a mutual fund, the chance of beating the market is actually lower than 50 percent each year, so one's odds are even worse than 1 in 32,768. By way of comparison, no Chinese mutual fund manager has ever managed to beat the market for more than five years in a row.

Miller's outstanding performance garnered him various accolades and the unofficial title "greatest investor of the decade." Nevertheless, he remained modest about his achievements and insisted that he managed to beat the market year in, year out largely because of the calendar effect and good fortune: "If every year ended at the end of November, instead of the end of December, then my winning streak may have ended a long time ago ... We have been very lucky. Our performance may not be entirely due to luck, but probably 95 percent [is] due to luck."[3]

That assessment proved astute, because in 2005 William Miller's luck ran out. In that year his fund trailed the market benchmark for the first time since 1991. Then, three years later, he aggressively increased his holdings in financial and real estate stocks just before the global financial crisis reached its full bloom. As a result, his fund lost 55 percent during 2008, greatly under-performing the market benchmark (which suffered a 37 percent loss). And that was not an isolated blip: Miller's fund under-performed the market benchmark every year from 2005 to 2011, aside from 2009. As a result, his fund's assets under management (AUM) shrank from a peak of more than 20 billion dollars to less than 3 billion in 2011, when he finally called it a day and retired.

Behavioral biases in mutual fund investment

Whenever I teach students about the case of William Miller, I always ask them if they would have invested in his fund in 1995, 2000, 2005, or 2010. Most of them admit that they would have poured money into the fund in 2005—clearly, with the benefit of hindsight, the worst year to do so.

Naive linear projection is one of the most prevalent mistakes that individual investors make, along with excessive trading. Similar to their misguided tendency to chase rising stocks, past performance has a massive effect on investors' mutual fund choices. In contrast to individual stock investment—where fundamental information, insider tips, and macroeconomic news all influence investors' decision making—most mutual fund investors fixate on past performance because they do not believe that the other factors have much bearing on mutual fund performance.

The behavioral pattern that lies behind such investment choices is known as "gamblers' fallacy" or "representativeness bias." Psychologists have established that gamblers tend to use a few previous gambling outcomes to predict their future gambling outcomes. For example, some choose to play a slot machine that has recently paid out in the belief that it is "loose" and therefore more likely to pay out again than the other machines. Other gamblers, in contrast, subscribe to the theory that a slot machine that has not paid out for a long time is more likely to pay out in the future, given that many previous gamblers have failed to make money from it, so the next one has a higher probability of cashing in.[4] Similarly, in gambling on basketball, many gamblers believe that a player who has performed well in the first few minutes will continue to perform well throughout the rest of the game.[5]

These behavioral patterns are manifestations of what Daniel Kahneman terms "representativeness bias"—human beings tend to use recent, salient, concrete examples in order to understand the universe and make predictions about the future. For example, psychologists have asked subjects to predict the outcome of a coin toss after witnessing one of two sequences: either OXOXXOOOXXOX or OOOOOOOOOOOO (where "O" represents heads and "X" represents tails). Although neither of these sequences can have any bearing on what happens with the next coin toss, subjects display much more confidence when predicting the outcome in the latter case, irrespective of whether they expect the heads sequence to continue or whether they believe that the coin must land on tails after so many consecutive heads.

This experiment highlights two common psychological patterns. First, human beings pay unjustifiably high attention to concrete examples that happen right in front of their eyes while simultaneously disregarding the basic law of probability. Second, most people do not fully understand the law of large numbers, wrongfully believing that probability holds true even in very small samples. To make matters even worse, many subjects modify their expectation or understanding of the law of probability on the basis of very limited visual evidence.

In line with this general psychological pattern, individual investors tend to chase mutual funds that can boast of outstanding past performance. They put little effort into assessing whether that outstanding performance is likely to continue or trying to understand why the fund achieved such high returns—for instance, was it through skill or luck?

The driving forces behind mutual fund returns: risk, style, skill, and luck

As discussed earlier, the primary reason why individual investors rely heavily on mutual funds' past performance to predict their future performance is because they do not understand the other factors that can influence fund performance. This section will discuss this topic and help investors achieve consistently good performance through investment in mutual funds.

Risk

Risk is always a dominant consideration when determining why a fund has succeeded or failed. A famous example from China is the Zhongyou Core Select Fund. This was one of the best-performing mutual funds in 2007 and one of the worst performing in 2008. The fund invested heavily in small cap stocks with high previous earnings growth and stock price appreciation. During the 2007 Chinese stock bubble, such speculative bets paid off handsomely, earning the fund spectacular returns, lucrative fees, and a prestigious reputation. However, when the bubble burst the following year, the same risky stocks dragged the fund down to the bottom of the pack.

In the world of investment and finance, there is a general trade-off between risk and return. Risky securities must generate unusually high returns in order to attract investors and mitigate their risk aversion. When the market rises, these risky stocks tend to rise higher than the market benchmark, but when the market falls, they tend to fall further. As a result, investors face the almost impossible task of predicting when the whole market will rise and when it will fall if they are to maximize their gains and minimize their losses. Zhongyou's very risky portfolio benefited from a rising market but then paid the price when the market started to fall. Unfortunately, many investors did not understand that risky portfolios are always susceptible to such volatile corrections, so they jumped into the fund after witnessing its outstanding performance in 2007, only to suffer considerable losses the following year.

Naturally, all mutual fund management companies broadcast full details of their outstanding years but remain reticent once the market has suffered a downturn. Hence, potential investors receive highly selective information that can often mislead them into believing that a very risky fund is certain to continue posting very impressive returns in the future.

Style

Different investors have various styles. For example, Fidelity's Peter Lynch favors growth stocks, while Wang Yawei, one of the most successful mutual fund managers in China, prefers small cap with good potential for restructuring, and Warren Buffett invests in stocks with simple business ideas and pricing power.

It is worth noting that similar types of stock tend to have similar performance and risk profiles. For example, the Chinese market has witnessed particularly strong growth in consumption, renewable energy, and state-owned enterprise reforms in specific periods. The question for mutual fund investors, however, is whether it is possible to predict the surging performance of a particular stock style or sector. Put differently, an investor may not know whether to stick with a fund manager who favors growth stocks or switch to one who prefers small cap companies.[6]

Similarly, some sell-side analysts are consistently bullish about the Chinese A-shares market while others are invariably bearish. And both groups can present evidence in support of their arguments. After all, given the market's perpetual fluctuations, almost every prediction comes true eventually. However, it is quite a leap to say that mutual fund managers deserve credit and adulation when their preferred stocks perform well over a specific period of time. It is important to keep in mind that every type of stock has its own life-cycle—it will out-perform its rivals during some periods and under-perform them during others. So if a mutual fund manager expects praise when his preferred stock type does well, he should accept criticism when it performs badly.

Although it is hard for mutual fund investors to switch style dramatically, fund management companies routinely market their funds with reference to the styles they favor. Indeed, some US mutual funds have changed their names in order to cater to retail investors' preference for particular investment styles. For example, many funds rebranded themselves to highlight that they had switched from large cap stocks to small cap stocks when the latter started to out-perform the former. Similarly, many funds started to feature the word "growth" in place of "value" in their titles during the late 1990s internet bubble in order to attract the new generation of ambitious retail investors.[7]

To draw investors' attention towards different stock types and sectors, many mutual fund companies gradually roll out index funds and exchange-traded funds that are linked to the performance of different industry sectors and investment types. Such funds passively track the performance of different stock types and charge relatively low fees. Therefore, they can serve as a more economical, safer alternative for investors who are interested in particular stock types or sectors and wish to avoid the uncertainty of investing in more costly mutual funds.[8]

Skill

After controlling for the variations in risk and luck across different mutual funds (many software packages and specialized service providers can help with this), comparing the funds' or individual fund managers' skill becomes much more meaningful.

In some circumstances, you might be wiser to invest in a fund that has just generated an annual return of 12 percent rather than one that has generated 20 percent, for the following reason. If the 20 percent fund has been investing in small stocks in a sector that has out-performed the market benchmark, then there is no reason to believe that the fund manager possesses any great skill. *Anybody* investing in such stocks over the same period would have recorded similarly impressive returns. By contrast, if the manager of the 12 percent fund has been investing in a sector that has fallen over the previous year, then he has a rare gift for finding needles in haystacks—companies that succeed despite the prevailing market conditions. *He* is the skillful investor, not the manager who earned an extra 8 percent.

Unfortunately, when thinking about investment returns, most retail investors concentrate solely on the headline figure, without taking risk, style, or skill into consideration. Hence, they also tend to fixate on a fund's past performance, and often pay a hefty price as a result.

Luck

If a mutual fund's performance cannot be traced to risk, style, or investment skills, then the chances are that it is due to pure luck. The problem with luck is that it does not always favor the same person. This goes some way to explaining why William Miller achieved such legendary performance between 1990 and 2005, but then very disappointing performance between 2006 and 2011. Because the returns generated by luck are unlikely to be achieved in the future, investors who are tempted to buy mutual funds on the basis of outstanding past performance that is due to luck will tend to suffer losses in the future.

We studied the ten best-performing mutual funds each year between 2006 and 2014, tracking which of them managed to repeat their success and gain a place in the top ten the following year. The results were disappointing. Over the eight-year study period, a particular fund achieved a place in the top ten for two years in a row on only four occasions.

Such results are not exceptional or specific to China. US researchers have conducted numerous studies over various evaluation periods—one year, five years, ten years—and have reached a very similar conclusion: mutual funds find it very difficult to repeat outstanding performance in subsequent years.[9]

How to invest in mutual funds

Given the above challenges facing individual investors who invest in mutual funds, most of them should probably consider investing in passively managed index funds and exchange-traded funds, which track the market's average performance for a relatively modest fee.

International studies have shown that actively managed mutual funds as a whole cannot out-perform the market. So, in any given year, although some individual investors will manage to pick mutual funds that out-perform the market, just as many or more will pick under-performing funds. This is a manifestation of the so-called "efficient market hypothesis," which stipulates that stock prices are typically correctly priced, which does not leave much room to make profits. Furthermore, mutual funds must abide by various regulations in terms of asset allocation, risk profile, and cash management, which limit their ability to pursue the highest possible returns.[10]

Therefore, individual investors should set realistic goals for their investments and allocate a considerable proportion of their portfolios to passively managed index funds and/or exchange-traded funds. This kind of passive investment approach should help individual investors avoid picking the wrong mutual funds at the wrong time. Similar to the mistakes that retail investors make when investing in individual stocks, fund investors often invest in the wrong funds at the wrong time.

The flow of money into mutual funds serves as a reliable negative indicator of market movement in China. The stock market peaked in 2007 and 2015, which coincided with peaks in the opening of new mutual fund accounts and the flow of money into the mutual fund industry, indicating that investors were chasing past returns and naively predicting that the high returns would continue into the future without properly considering the risks and patterns of the market. The over-confidence that plagues individual stock investors also hinders individual investors in mutual funds. Investors tend to be far too confident about their own information and ability, which eventually leads to excessive trading and disappointing returns from their mutual fund investments.

Moreover, passive mutual fund investment reduces the fees that individual investors have to pay to fund managers, which means that they get to keep more of the returns they make. Chinese fund management companies continue to charge a total of more than 10 billion RMB per year in fees even during bear markets, when the investors in those funds inevitably lose some of their investment. Yet our research indicates that investors often pay no attention to the fees they will be charged when choosing their mutual funds. Instead, in line with investors in many other markets, they chase the funds that can boast of outstanding recent performance, even if those funds charge fees that are 50 percent higher than the industry standard. Such investors need to understand the extent to which management fees can erode their net returns, so the very least they should do is choose a low-cost alternative.

Notes

1. www.amac.org.cn/xhdt/zxdt/391463.shtml.
2. Liao, L., Zhang, W., and Zhu, N. 2012. *The Performance of Chinese Mutual Fund Investors*. Working paper, Shanghai Advanced Institute of Finance.
3. www.baltimoresun.com/business/bs-bz-miller-20130810-story.html.
4. Zheng, L. 1999. Is Money Smart? A Study of Mutual Fund Investors' Fund Selection Ability. *Journal of Finance*, 54(3): 901–933.
5. Camerer, C.F. 1989. Does the Basketball Market Believe in the Hot Hand? *American Economic Review*, 79(5): 1257–1261.
6. Sharpe, W.F. 1966. Mutual Fund Performance. *Journal of Business*, 39(1): 119–138.
7. www.fep.up.pt/investigacao/cempre/actividades/sem_fin/sem_fin_01/PAPERS_PDF/paper_sem_fin_8mai03.pdf.
8. Carhart, M.M. 1997. On Persistence in Mutual Fund Performance. *Journal of Finance*, 52(1): 57–82.
9. Jensen, M.C. 1968. The Performance of Mutual Funds in the Period 1945–1964. *Journal of Finance*, 23(2): 389–416.
10. Ippolito, R.A. 1989. Efficiency with Costly Information: A Study of Mutual Fund Performance, 1965–1984. *Quarterly Journal of Economics*, 104(1): 1–23.

6
IRRATIONAL MIND

Look at Figure 6.1 and decide which of the two tables is higher. Now look at Figure 6.2 and decide which of the two white lines is longer.

In fact, both tables are the same height and both lines are the same length.

Few people believe that the two tables are the same height when first looking at them, but then they measure them with a ruler and learn the truth. And the same thing happens with the white lines.

Both of these pictures are used by psychological researchers in order to show the limitations of people's cognitive processes, especially visual perception. The old adage may say "Seeing is believing," but these pictures prove that what one sees with one's own eyes may not result in an accurate understanding of the truth.[1]

According to the behavioral economist Daniel Kahneman, human beings think in two parallel ways: fast and slow. Fast thinking is more spontaneous but less accurate, whereas slow thinking is more careful but cumbersome. Fast thinking is more intuitive whereas slow thinking is more rational. However, as Kahneman shows in his large body of research, human beings are poor at switching between these two types of thinking and often use fast thinking when more careful and deliberate decision making would be more beneficial.[2]

Figure 6.3 is often the most surprising test of all. Look at the image and decide whether Square A or Square B is darker.

Most people think that this question is preposterous and reply immediately that Square A is obviously darker than Square B. In fact, they are identical shades of gray. Adding a benchmark in the form of two parallel lines of the same shade of gray helps people to see the truth (Figure 6.4). Alternatively, if one were to remove the two squares from the chequerboard context, almost everyone would see that they were the same shade of gray.

Investors' financial decision making is not too different from this example. They have to process information in a highly dynamic and often uncertain environment

Have a look, if you will, at these two tables

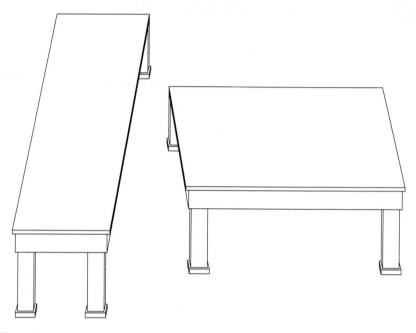

Figure 6.1

Source Shepard, R.N. 1990. *Mind Sights: Original Visual Illusions, Ambiguities, and Other Anomalies, with a Commentary on the Play of Mind in Perception and Art.* New York: WH Freeman

and try to discern the truth in order to make the best investment decisions. The chequerboard example illustrates that our decision making can be dramatically influenced by context, and how easy it is to reach incorrect decisions.

Now look at Figure 6.5 for five to ten seconds. Then close your eyes and try to remember what is in the picture.

Many people have a vague recollection of three incomplete circles and three incomplete triangles, but even more recall seeing a large white inverted triangle. Even though this large white inverted triangle is not defined by any border, a majority of people are left with a vivid impression of it.

Once again, there is an analogy in investment. People read books, glance through newspapers and magazines, watch TV, chat with their friends, and subscribe to investment newsletters in order to garner more information about capital markets and investment. However, they often have no way of knowing if the information they receive is true or if it will help their investment decisions. This is precisely the challenge that most investors face. They are bombarded with increasingly large amounts of information, which makes it almost impossible for them to decide what is true and useful. Indeed, they are often misled by false information or even act on information that never really existed in the first place, like the large white inverted triangle in Figure 6.5.

Figure 6.2

Source Seckel, A. 2006. *The Ultimate Book of Optical Illusions.* New York: Sterling.

Figure 6.3

Source Seckel, A. 2006. *The Ultimate Book of Optical Illusions.* New York: Sterling.

Figure 6.4
Source Seckel, A. 2006. *The Ultimate Book of Optical Illusions*. New York: Sterling.

Finally, look at Figure 6.6. What do you see? At first, some people see a rabbit looking to the right while others see a duck looking to the left. After a while, though, most people are able to discern both the rabbit and the duck. In other words, when looking at an identical source of information, two individuals might initially reach very different conclusions and then make very different decisions on the basis of those conclusions.

The same phenomenon occurs in stock investment. On receipt of a particular stock tip, one person may think it offers a once-in-a-lifetime opportunity, whereas another may sense a trap and potential disaster. Moreover, one person may make two very different decisions on the basis of a single piece of information. For instance, they might buy a stock one day then have second thoughts and sell it the next, even though they have received no new information in the interim.

Over the past few decades, psychological research has revolutionized the way in which economists and financial economists conduct their own research. Behavioral finance has grown tremendously over the past three decades. Professors Vernon Smith and Daniel Kahneman won the 2002 Nobel Prize for Economics for their foundational contribution to behavioral economics and behavioral finance. Professor Robert Shiller received the 2013 Nobel Prize for Economics for his work that links human behavior to asset price theory, and further research has shown that investors' behavioral patterns have a significant impact on asset price and market fluctuation.

Figure 6.5
Source Seckel, A. 2006. *The Ultimate Book of Optical Illusions.* New York: Sterling.

The links between human behavior and investment decision making are often explored through laboratory experiments. In one classic experiement, a group of people are asked to rate their driving skills and place themselves in one of the following five categories:

1. The best 20 percent (80–100 percentile)
2. The relatively better 20 percent (60–80 percentile)
3. The average 20 percent (40–60 percentile)
4. The relatively poor 20 percent (20–40 percentile)
5. The worst 20 percent (0–20 percentile)[3]

When conducting this experiment on 51 of my students, 16 felt that they belonged in Group 1, another 15 students placed themselves in Group 2, 11 felt their driving skills were average, 5 believed they were relatively poor drivers, and 1 admitted

Figure 6.6
Source Seckel, A. 2006. *The Ultimate Book of Optical Illusions.* New York: Sterling.

that she was probably among the worst drivers on the road (the remaining 3 students could not drive).

This is probably one of the most replicated tests in behavioral economics and behavioral finance. Researchers have changed the subject to ask about everything from IQ, to appearance, to popularity, but the results are always broadly similar: when asked to make a subjective judgment about their relative standing within a group, people usually over-estimate themselves. This is sometimes known as the "Lake Wobegon effect" after the fictional town that features in Garrison Keiller's radio show, where "all the men are strong and all the women are beautiful." The degree of over-confidence tends to be rather higher in the West, but the same pattern is still evident in China and Japan.

Some subjects in these experiments argue that they do not really know the other participants' skills. But that is exactly the point of the experiment: the subjects are asked to judge *their own* ability in a context of information asymmetry.

Even when people do not have much understanding of the risks of investment, they tend to use the limited knowledge and experience they do possess in order to make important decisions. For example, when investors are asked what they would do with a fund that has lost 1.3 percent, 0.6 percent, and 1.5 percent in each of the past three years, most say they would cut their investment or at least not invest any more money in the fund. Similarly, when investors are asked what they would do with a fund that has made profits of 1.3 percent, 0.6 percent, and 1.5 percent in each of the past three years, most say they would increase their investment in the fund. As previous chapters have shown, investors focus on what has happened in order to make predictions about what will happen in the future while ignoring important fundamental questions, such as what caused the fund to make or lose money over the past three years.

This is an important aspect of investor behavior. Instead of searching for more detailed information that would help them make more informed investment decisions, most investors believe that they have the ability to foresee the future and remain convinced that the limited information at their disposal (often no more than the fund's end-of-year balance sheet) allows them to make accurate decisions.

Context has a similarly large impact on human decision making. For instance, when subjects in experiments are asked to estimate the number of African countries in the UN, those who recently watched a basketball game (in which both teams probably scored in the region of 100 points) tend to make much higher guesses than those who watched a baseball game (in which both teams probably scored fewer than 10 runs). Two seemingly unrelated activities seem to influence each other, suggesting that context has a profound impact on human decision making. To some extent, investors who look at past returns are no different from the experimental subjects who watched a baseball game or a basketball game—they are all under the strong influence of context without realizing it.[4]

Another series of experiments illustrates how people may respond to identical gains or losses in radically different ways, once again highlighting the complexity of human decision making and especially financial decision making. Subjects were asked to imagine that they had received a 200-dollar ticket for a theatre show, a vase worth 200 dollars, or 200 dollars in cash just before setting off to see the aforementioned show. Group A were then told to imagine that they subsequently lost the ticket; Group B were told to imagine that they broke the vase; and Group C were told to imagine that they lost the cash. All three groups were then asked whether they would still go to see the show. About a third of the Group A subjects chose to stay at home, even though they were informed that they had more than enough money to replace the lost ticket and that they could buy one easily at the box office. In contrast, no subjects from Group B or Group C changed their decision to see the show because they had broken the vase or lost the cash.

Given that the ticket, the vase, and the cash are all worth 200 dollars, this experiment suggests that human beings care about more than the simple monetary value of an object—sentiment and psychological attachment play important roles, too. This finding sharply contradicts the over-simplified assumptions that neo-classical economics holds about human beings' rationality. It also goes some way to explaining why traditional academic financial research has such trouble when trying to determine why financial markets behave as they do.

The above experiments provide valuable glimpses into how people behave and suggest that such behavioral patterns may have a profound impact on investors' decision making. Developments in technology and research methodology mean that psychological and behavioral science researchers are now less reliant on laboratory experiments. Instead, they are gaining new insights through their use of modern methods, such as magnetic resonance imaging (MRI) and neuron tracking. Experiments with MRI scanners have revealed that one part of the brain is particularly active when stock traders are trading. Moreover, that part of the brain is also unusually active when schizophrenics suffer episodes of mental illness. The researchers concluded that the similarities between the traders' and the schizophrenics' brain activity are linked to the way in which the human brain responds to risk. Successful traders are trained to be indifferent to risk in the face of market fluctuations, while schizophrenics suffer from an inability to assess the inherent risks of various types of behavior.[5]

Psychological research has revealed that investment decision making is far more complex than traditional finance research has assumed, and future studies must incorporate the recent findings of psychology and the behavioral sciences if they are to gain a full understanding of how the financial markets operate.

As earlier chapters have indicated, it is not only retail investors and mutual fund managers who are influenced by behavioral bias and their own limitations; senior company executives and government officials also suffer from these counter-productive behavioral traits. Given these shared behavioral patterns and limitations, it is important to understand human nature before one even attempts to understand what causes stock market volatility, housing market bubbles, and the pattern of boom and bust in the global economy.[6]

Notes

1. Shepard, R.N. 1990. Mind Sights: Original Visual Illusions, Ambiguities, and Other Anomalies, with a Commentary on the Play of Mind in Perception and Art. New York: WH Freeman.
2. Seckel, A. 2006. *The Ultimate Book of Optical Illusions*. New York: Sterling.
3. Tversky, A. and Kahneman, D. 1974. Judgment under Uncertainty: Heuristics and Biases. *Science*, 185: 1124–1130.
4. Tversky, A. and Kahneman, D. 1974. Judgment under Uncertainty: Heuristics and Biases. *Science*, 185: 1124–1130; Tversky, A. and Kahneman, D. 1975. *Judgment under Uncertainty: Heuristics and Biases*. Dordrecht: Springer.
5. Kuhnen, C.M. and Knutson, B. 2005. The Neural Basis of Financial Risk Taking. *Neuron*, 47(5): 763–770.
6. Thaler, R.H. and Sunstein, C.R. 2008. *Nudge: Improving Decisions about Health, Wealth, and Happiness*. New Haven, CT: Yale University Press.

7

BEHAVIORAL BIASES AND INVESTMENT DECISION MAKING

Over-confidence

Building upon the previous chapters, this chapter primarily deals with how human behavioral biases influence their financial decision making and investment performance.

It is undeniable that most human beings are over-confident in their own abilities. However, it is one thing to be over-confident in one's driving skills or popularity, and quite another to allow one's over-confidence to influence one's investment decisions and performance.

Let us review the driving skills study (see Chapter 6), which revealed that about 80 percent of subjects believe that their skills are above average. Even if such an assessment is extremely biased, it is unlikely either to harm or help other road users. After all, the outcome of one's own driving does not depend heavily on the driving skills of other drivers.

However, investment is different. It is a "competitive sport" in which one's own performance depends heavily on the performance of others. In short, investment is in some way a "zero sum" game. Put simply, no new wealth is created in a financial market—all the market does is redistribute existing wealth from one party to another. So, if someone makes money from their investments, someone else has to lose money. Similarly, if someone loses money, all of that money is pocketed by rival investors. Not a penny more, not a penny less.[1] This is where over-confidence assumes vital importance.

Imagine that you enter a casino to play poker and you are offered the option of playing against a table of novices or a group of world champions. You would probably choose to play against the novices, as you would assume that you would have a greater chance of winning against these inevitably weaker opponents. Similarly, if the only option were to play against world champions, you might choose to leave the casino without playing a single hand.

The same logic should apply to investing in financial markets. Each potential investor should compare their own ability with that of their rivals. If they feel that their ability is superior, then they should engage in active investment; otherwise, they should look for another market or forget about active investment altogether. This is the only sensible course of action, because, if an investor's ability is inferior to the market average, then he has a greater chance of losing money to other investors than winning money from them.

In this regard, securities and poker are quite similar in that the law of large number applies. Some retail investors get lucky when they first start trading, which gives them the impression that they have a knack for investment. However, most of them gradually learn the true nature of their investment abilities and lose what they made initially.[2]

To make matters worse for retail investors, it could be argued that stock market investment is even worse than a zero sum game because fees, commissions, and taxes are all incurred during trading, so money is transferred to stockbrokers and exchanges irrespective of whether the investor wins or loses. Consequently, the money that investors redistribute among themselves is always less than what they, as a group, put into the market.

Furthermore, gambling is generally a game of chance, whereas investment is heavily dependent on one's skills and sources of information. Some investors—such as institutions and professional fund managers—have access to high-quality information as well as considerable skill and experience, which means they are likely to make money rather than lose it. On the other side of the same coin, retail investors lack these advantages, so they are more likely to lose money (as someone must lose if someone else is to gain).

Unlike the gaming industry, which most governments do not encourage (for instance, Singaporean citizens have to pay a hefty entrance fee in order to enter casinos in their own country), stock markets are widely publicized and hotly debated around the world. Innumerable TV channels, stockbrokers, and fund managers compete with each other to attract potential investors' attention and boost their own cash flow and profits. This only encourages investors' over-confidence in their own investment abilities. As we have seen in the driving skills experiment, about 80 percent of people believe that they are better than average with respect to any particular skill, which of course is a mathematical impossibility. Moreover, this is especially true in stock market investment, given that retail investors compete against far more experienced professional investors who can devote more time to studying the market and receive better information than the amateurs. Therefore, potential investors who suspect that they do not possess the necessary skills to compete against the professionals need to think very carefully about whether it is a good idea for them to invest in the stock market.

Sometimes, of course, a stock market *will* generate wealth for more than just the highly skilled few, largely as a consequence of economic development. Moreover, when a market is exceptionally bullish, every investor will make money and nobody will lose. However, in such contexts, it is important to remember that simply making a profit should not be the benchmark by which to evaluate an investor's "success," given that the whole market is booming. Instead, one should assess the success or failure of an investor on the basis of whether she has out-performed the market index. If we evaluate investors by this standard, the zero sum concept comes into play again in the sense that any money that is made over and above the general market performance must come from investors who have performed worse than the market index.

Research in the US and China indicates that only 5–10 percent of retail investors have the ability to out-perform the market consistently over a long period of time (five to ten years), whereas 30–40 percent of retail investors consistently under-perform the market. The rest achieve returns that are quite close to the market benchmark.[3] Nevertheless, the Federal Reserve's Survey of Consumer Finance and a similar survey conducted by Tsinghua University reveal that large proportions of retail investors in the US and China, respectively, believe that they achieve above-market performance.[4] The reason for this collective delusion is that many investors do not have a true grasp of their own investment performance. First, they do not keep accurate records of how much money their own stocks have gained or lost. Second, they do not know the average market performance over the same period, so they cannot compare their portfolios with a reliable benchmark.

Those retail investors who acknowledge that they cannot out-perform the market tend to opt for affordable and easy diversification through index funds and exchange-traded funds (ETFs). Of course, such funds, which tend to have lower management and incentive fees than mutual funds, generate higher net returns for individual investors, all else being equal. And research indicates that the mutual fund industry does not out-perform the market in general, so index funds and ETFs *will* usually achieve gross returns that are equal to (or better than) those of mutual funds. This rule holds true in China, as it does almost everywhere else.[5] If mutual funds generally fail to out-perform the market, why would a shrewd investor pay mutual fund management fees of 1.5 percent when she could pay a far smaller percentage to an index fund or an ETF *and* guarantee herself average market returns?[6]

ETFs and index funds charge half (or even less) than mutual funds in management fees, so they are more affordable options for retail investors.[7] Given that their primary task is to track the market precisely, they also save investors the agonizing task of deciding which mutual fund to choose. We have already seen that choosing a profitable mutual fund is just as challenging as choosing a profitable stock, so, inevitably, most retail investors lack the skill to make the correct decision.

Finally, it is worth mentioning again that over-confidence is a common human trait. According to psychological and physiological research, over-confidence helps create a positive self-image, which in turn can maintain an optimistic outlook and good health.[8] For example, studies have found that HIV-positive patients who have a positive attitude towards their health tend to survive longer than those who do not. On the other hand, as we have seen in previous chapters, over-confidence can also result in cursory and careless investment. Retail investors often take investment lightly and over-estimate their ability to manage the situation.[9] This is partly related to the "illusion of control," which leads people to the false belief that they have control over the outcome purely because they have control over the process.

Over-confidence may also lead investors to set unrealistically high investment targets that are impossible to attain. This tendency can cause investors with reasonably good investment ability to subject themselves to unjustified self-criticism because they have chosen the wrong benchmark against which to assess themselves. More ominously, less skilled investors who set unrealistically high targets may be tempted to make ever more risky investments as they attempt to reach their goal, which almost always ends in disaster.[10]

According to Daniel Kahneman, people often under-estimate the time and effort that are required to complete certain tasks. Furthermore, he argues that human beings have a tendency to over-estimate future benefits (investment returns) and under-estimate future costs (risks).[11] This may be related to the fact that people tend to ignore the fact that they are over-confident because that very over-confidence makes them feel better about themselves. Some commentators have suggested that this tendency explains why so many corporate mergers and acquisitions prove much more difficult than either the acquirer or the target originally expected.[12]

Thinking framework

In this section, we will discuss how thinking frameworks influence investment decisions. First, though, let's do a little experiment.

Ask yourself which kind of mouse has two feet.

The correct answer is "Mickey Mouse."

Next, ask yourself which kind of duck has two feet?

The correct answer is "Every duck."

People often answer "Donald Duck," which is totally understandable, given that the previous answer was "Mickey Mouse."

This little test highlights a very common and important aspect of most people's thinking process. The framework within which one thinks has far more influence on one's decision making than most people realize.

Framework is also crucially important when making investment decisions. An investor's decision to purchase a particular stock may be heavily influenced by which newspaper he read that morning, which company one of his trusted friends recommended over coffee, or whether another stock has just reached its historical high or low (or daily price movement limit in China). Even though none of these provides much information about a stock's fundamentals, all three have the power to persuade an investor to buy a particular stock.

Once a framework has formed, it is surprisingly difficult to amend. As we saw in Chapter 6, whether you have 200 dollars in cash, a ticket that is worth 200 dollars, or a 200-dollar vase can have an unexpectedly large influence on your decision making. People do not respond simply to monetary differences; they also care about the form in which they possess that money. Numerous psychological experiments have shown that people respond to gains and losses in distinctive patterns. Loss aversion—an individual's desire to avoid suffering any sort of loss— is a very strong psychological trait that is critical in understanding certain aspects of human behavior. For example, marketing experts have learned that it is easy to bundle unnecessary items to an already expensive purchase. Someone who is buying a 50,000-dollar car will normally not fret about spending another 5,000 on the "premium package," which includes a sun roof, ceramic brakes, and keyless ignition, even though they have little use for any of those features. Similarly, people are far more likely to order an over-priced dessert after treating themselves to an expensive dinner. If consumers view expenditure as "loss," than a little extra on top of an initial significant loss seems far more palatable than several individual smaller losses that total the same amount.[13]

One very common manifestation of loss aversion in investment is the "disposition effect"—namely, investors' tendency to sell winning stocks too soon and hold on to losing stocks for too long. Selling losing stocks creates such psychological discomfort that many investors choose to stick their heads in the sand and pretend that the falling shares will eventually bounce back, even though experience should tell them that they rarely do.

Even after suffering individual stock losses, investors still try to look for the silver lining in their portfolios. For instance, if an investor has bought one winning stock and five losers, he will tend to focus on the winning stock and use it as evidence for his "superior" investment ability. Such biased responses to gains and losses, and asymmetrical reactions to winning and losing stocks, often result in retail investors boasting about their investment successes but remaining silent about their failures. Of course, this may well persuade potential investors that stock market investment is a fool-proof way to make easy money.

Studies also show that people are highly sensitive to the context in which gains and losses are presented. Kahneman and Tversky provide a classic example of this:

> Imagine that the United States is preparing for the outbreak of an unusual Asian disease, which is expected to kill 600 people. Two alternative programs to combat the disease have been proposed. Assume that the exact scientific estimates of the consequences of the programs are as follows:
>
> - If Program A is adopted, 200 people will be saved
> - If Program B is adopted, there is a one-third probability that 600 people will be saved and a two-thirds probability that no people will be saved
>
> Which of the two programs would you favor?
>
> In this version of the problem, a substantial majority of respondents favor Program A, indicating risk aversion.
>
> Other respondents, selected at random, receive a question in which the same cover story is followed by a different description of the options:

- If Program A★ is adopted, 400 people will die
- If Program B★ is adopted, there is a one-third probability that nobody will die and a two-thirds probability that 600 people will die

A clear majority of respondents now favor Program B★, the risk-seeking option.

Although there is no substantive difference between the versions, they evidently evoke different associations and evaluations.

This is easiest to see in the certain option, because outcomes that are certain are over-weighted relative to outcomes of high or intermediate probability. Thus, the certainty of saving people is disproportionately attractive, and the certainty of deaths is disproportionately aversive. These immediate affective responses respectively favor A over B, and B★ over A★.

The question of how to determine whether two decision problems are "the same" or different does not have a general answer. To avoid this issue, [we] restricted framing effects to discrepancies between choice problems that decision makers, upon reflection, consider effectively identical. The Asian disease problem passes this test: respondents who are asked to compare the two versions almost always conclude that the same action should be taken in both. Observers agree that it would be frivolous to let a superficial detail of formulation determine a choice that has life and death consequences.[14]

A few years later, Kahneman devised another experiment.[15] Imagine that you are facing a pair of concurrent decisions. First examine both decisions, then make your choices.

- Decision 1: Choose between:
  A. Sure gain of $240
  B. 25 percent chance of gaining $1,000 and 75 percent chance of gaining nothing

- Decision 2: Choose between:
  C. Sure loss of $750
  D. 75 percent chance of losing $1,000 and 25 percent chance of losing nothing

Most people, looking at both decisions concurrently, choose A and D.
But now consider another choice, this time between:

AD. 25 percent chance of winning $240 and 75 percent chance of losing $760
BC. 25 percent chance of winning $250 and 75 percent chance of losing $750

Clearly, any sane person would choose BC as it seems better than option AD in both respects. However, AD is precisely the combination of options A and D, while BC is the combination of the previously rejected options B and C. We act in this way because the choice between A and B is a choice between a certain outcome and an uncertain outcome, and the same is true for the choice between C and D. When faced with certain gains and certain losses—especially certain losses—human beings will make unusual choices in order to avoid the losses. This is why the insurance industry is so profitable—it exploits people's strong desire to eliminate any unwelcome possibilities.[16]

One implication of these behavioral patterns is that one should always try to leave open the possibility of a positive outcome for counterparties during negotiations. This makes it much easier to reach an agreement.

In addition to their responses to gains and losses, people are sensitive to the relative magnitude of those gains and losses. In an experiment, Dan Ariely offered two groups the opportunity to purchase an item. The members of the first group were told that there would be a "25 dollars off" promotion on a piece of furniture worth 100 dollars the following day. The members of the second group were told that there would be a "25 dollars off" promotion on a computer worth 1,000 dollars the following day. Both groups were then asked whether they would purchase the item today, or wait until tomorrow to take advantage of the promotion. Although the savings would be identical for both groups, most members of the first group decided to postpone their purchase whereas most members of the second group chose to buy the computer immediately. This indicates that people tend to put absolute figures in relative frameworks—an identical saving is framed in two very different contexts (a 25 percent saving against a 2.5 percent saving)—which can have a significant influence on their decision making.[17]

Therefore, psychological research has shown that framing an event as positive or negative, and framing it as certain or uncertain, can have profound implications for how individuals respond to such events and reach decisions about them.

Representativeness bias

As discussed earlier, Daniel Kahneman and Amos Tversky have explored a particularly interesting human behavioral pattern which they term "representativeness bias." When we make decisions based on representativeness, we are likely to make more errors and tend to over-estimate the likelihood that something will occur. An event is no more likely to occur simply because it is representative, so one should always take substantive information based on large samples into consideration before reaching a decision.[18]

Kahneman and Tversky presented the following character study to college students and asked for their opinions:

> Tom W. is of high intelligence, although lacking in true creativity. He has a need for order and clarity, and for neat and tidy systems in which every detail finds its appropriate place. His writing is rather dull and mechanical, occasionally enlivened by somewhat corny puns and by flashes of imagination of the sci-fi type. He has a strong drive for competence. He seems to feel

little sympathy for other people and does not enjoy interacting with others. Self-centered, he nonetheless has a deep moral sense.[19]

Most of the students guessed that Tom was probably an engineering major, even though there were relatively few engineering students at the school where the study was conducted. They based their decisions on representativeness, ignoring more pertinent information, such as the small number of engineering students.[20]

> The representativeness heuristic is the tendency to judge the frequency or likelihood of an event by the extent to which it resembles the typical case. For example, in a series of 10 coin tosses, most people judge the series HHTTHTHTTH to be more likely than the series HHHHHHHHHH (where H is heads and T is tails), even though both series are equally likely. The reason is that the first series looks more random than the second series. It "represents" our idea of what a random series should look like.[21]

These behavioral patterns explain why individual investors often pick the stock or mutual fund that has performed well recently. They employ the simple HHHHHHH projection when assessing stock or mutual fund performance, even though stock prices usually follow what is known as a "random walk." Unsurprisingly, this means they are often left disappointed when past winners do not repeat their former gains, and indeed often turn into losers.

Similar thinking may also help explain why so many investors jump into the stock market just as it reaches its peak. The market's past success generates increasing confidence among potential investors that the gains "must" continue. Unfortunately, such investors often fall victim to "representativeness heuristics" and lose considerable sums by timing their entry into the market at the worst possible moment.

Mood

Contrary to the assumptions of neo-classical finance theory, investors' mood seems to have a strong influence on their investment decisions and indeed on stock prices. For example, researchers have found that the stock market often falls by about 0.5 percentage points when the country's team loses in the final of a major sporting event, such as the Football World Cup. The explanation is simple: many investors, especially male investors, are sports fans who are left miserable by the national team's defeat and mope around for a day or two before turning their attention back to the stock market.[22]

Behavioral finance research also suggests that the weather can influence stock market performance. Over the past 70 years, the US stock market has performed 0.2–0.3 percent better on sunny days than it has on overcast days. Such findings are especially surprising given that the weather in New York City has no influence on the United States macro economy or corporate earnings. Nor can it have much influence on the mood of the majority of retail investors, most of whom do not live in New York. Yet the pattern is undeniable, and it is not limited to the New York Stock Exchange: 85 percent of 40 stock exchanges located in mid-latitude cities around the world experienced something similar during the twentieth century.[23]

In light of this, we conducted a follow-up study and found that the bid–ask spread increases on cloudy days. Our conclusion was that the market makers, who *do* live and work in New York City, are psychologically influenced by that city's weather.[24]

Similarly, seasonal time adjustment also affects investor behavior and asset prices. Researchers have found that stock markets tend to perform particularly badly in the week after daylight saving begins and ends. Given that there is no evidence of unusual patterns in the economy or corporate earnings at such times, the conclusion is that investors' schedules are disturbed by the time changes, which affects their mood and level of risk aversion, which in turn influences stock prices.[25]

Similarly, lunar phase, magnetic fields, and even unusual solar activity are all widely believed to influence human psychology and behavior, so they all probably have some sort of effect on asset prices.

Notes

1 Liao, L., Li, Z., Zhang, W., and Zhu, N. 2013. Exercise to Lose Money? Irrational Exercise Behavior from the Chinese Warrants Market. *Journal of Futures Markets*. Retrieved from www.amac.org.cn/xhdt/zxdt/391463.shtml.
2 Liao, L., Li, Z., Zhang, W., and Zhu, N. 2010. Security Supply and Bubbles: A Natural Experiment from the Chinese Warrants Market. Working paper, Shanghai Advanced Institute of Finance.
3 Coval, J., Hirshleifer, D., and Shumway, T. 2005. Can Individual Investors Beat the Market? Working paper, Harvard University. Retrieved from https://papers.ssrn.com/sol3/papers.cfm?abstract-id=364000.
4 Liao, L., Li, Z., Zhang, W., and Zhu, N. 2013. Exercise to Lose Money? Irrational Exercise Behavior from the Chinese Warrants Market. *Journal of Futures Markets*. Retrieved from www.amac.org.cn/xhdt/zxdt/391463.shtml.
5 Malkiel, B.G. 1995. Returns from Investing in Equity Mutual Funds 1971 to 1991. *Journal of Finance*, 50(2): 549–572.
6 Ippolito, R.A. 1989. Efficiency with Costly Information: A Study of Mutual Fund Performance, 1965–1984. *Quarterly Journal of Economics*, 104(1): 1–23.
7 Sirri, E.R. and Tufano, P. 1998. Costly Search and Mutual Fund Flows. *Journal of Finance*, 53(5): 1589–1622; Jain, P.C. and Wu, J.S. 2000. Truth in Mutual Fund Advertising: Evidence on Future Performance and Fund Flows. *Journal of Finance*, 55(2): 937–958.
8 Taleb, N. 2010. *The Black Swan*. New York: Random House; Taleb, N. 2012. *Antifragile: Things that Gain from Disorder*. New York: Random House.
9 Adams, P. A. and Adams, J.K. 1960. Confidence in the Recognition and Reproduction of Words Difficult to Spell. *American Journal of Psychology*, 73(4): 544–552.
10 Johnson, D.D.P. 2004. *Overconfidence and War: The Havoc and Glory of Positive Illusions*. Cambridge, MA: Harvard University Press.
11 Kahneman, D. and Tversky, A. 1979. Intuitive Prediction: Biases and Corrective Procedures. *TIMS Studies in Management Science*, 12: 313–327.
12 Lovallo, D. and Kahneman, D. 2003. Delusions of Success: How Optimism Undermines Executives' Decisions. *Harvard Business Review*, 81(7): 56–63.
13 Wertenbroch, K. and Dhar, R. 2000. Consumer Choice between Hedonic and Utilitarian Goods. *Journal of Marketing Research*, 37(1): 60–71. See also: http://www.journals.marketingpower.com/doi/abs/10.1509/jmkr.37.1.60.18718.

14 http://www.nobelprize.org/nobel_prizes/economic-sciences/laureates/2002/kahnemann-lecture.pdf.
15 Kahneman, D. 2013. *Thinking Fast and Slow*. New York: Farrar, Straus and Giroux.
16 http://www.kevincoffey.com/travel/travel_insurance_should_i_get_it.htm.
17 Ariely, D. 2009. *Predictably Irrational: The Hidden Forces that Shape our Decisions*. New York: Harper.
18 Kahneman, D. and Tversky, A. 1972. Subjective Probability: A Judgment of Representativeness. *Cognitive Psychology*, 3(3): 430–454; Kahneman, D. and Tversky, D. 1972. Subjective Probability: A Judgment of Representativeness. In Kahneman, D., Slovic, P., and Tversky, D., *Judgment under Uncertainty: Heuristics and Biases*. Cambridge: Cambridge University Press.
19 http://psiexp.ss.uci.edu/research/teaching/Tversky_Kahneman_1974.pdf.
20 Kahneman, D., Slovic, P., and Tversky, D. *Judgment under Uncertainty: Heuristics and Biases*. Cambridge: Cambridge University Press.
21 http://psiexp.ss.uci.edu/research/teaching/Tversky_Kahneman_1974.pdf.
22 Edmans, A., Garcia, D., and Norli, Ø. 2007. Sports Sentiment and Stock Returns. *Journal of Finance*, 62(4): 1967–1998.
23 Hirshleifer, D. and Shumway, T. 2003. Good Day Sunshine: Stock Returns and the Weather. *Journal of Finance*, 58(3): 1009–1032.
24 Goetzmann, W.N. and Zhu, N. 2005. Rain or Shine: Where is the Weather Effect? *European Financial Management*, 11(5): 559–578.
25 Kamstra, M.J., Kramer, L.A., and Levi, M.D. 2003. Winter Blues: A SAD Stock Market Cycle. *American Economic Review*, 93(1): 324–343.

8
DIFFICULT HISTORY

Ray Dalio, the founder of Bridgewater, one of the largest hedge fund management companies in the world, once asked Charles Munger, the legendary investment partner of Warren Buffett, how he might become a better investor. He was told, "Read history, read history, read history." Similarly, there is an old saying in China that "Reading history makes you smart."

This chapter will discuss several famous bubble events from global financial history, each of which not only brought turmoil to the economy but had a profound impact on political stability and society.

The interesting thing about bubbles is that even though they seem incredible and stupendous with the benefit of hindsight, those who live through them remain fully convinced about their sustainability right up to the moment when they burst. In the examples that follow, we will see how excessive liquidity, novel concepts, implicit governmental support, and a lack of investor irrationality often combine to cause bubbles.

Tulip mania

Tulip mania is one of the earliest documented bubble events in financial history. Tulips were introduced to the Netherlands from Persia in the seventeenth century. This coincided with the former's rise to great power status, which was due primarily to the Dutch people's use of incorporation and the stock market to amass social wealth, which in turn was used to fund the exploration and colonization of other parts of the world.

At first, tulips were prized but otherwise unremarkable flowers, but then, in 1636, something extraordinary happened. The price of individual tulip bulbs started to escalate and quickly reached a peak of some 6,000 guilders for a particularly rare specimen. To put this into perspective, the average annual wage in the Netherlands at the time ranged between 200 and 400 guilders, and an average townhouse in Amsterdam cost about 300 guilders. According to Simon Schama, a "viceroy" tulip bulb was exchanged for "two last of wheat and four of rye, four fat oxen, eight pigs, a dozen sheep, two ox heads of wine, four tons of butter, a thousand pounds of cheese, a bed, some clothing, and a silver beaker" with a total value of some 2,500 guilders.[1]

Why were tulips so desirable, and why was the speculation on them so frenetic? First of all, lots of money flooded into the Netherlands as the country became the economic and financial center of the Western Hemisphere. And this process accelerated as the Dutch founded the world's first stock exchange and the number of listed companies increased. In other words, there was a surplus of cash and numerous potential investors who were looking for ways to invest it. Second, as a newly introduced species, tulips were viewed as extraordinarily beautiful and rare, so possessing one came to symbolize success and prosperity among the upper classes, opening the door for investment and speculation. Another interesting feature of tulips is that the bulbs must be buried underground before the next spring, which created information asymmetry between supply and demand.

Moreover, many contracts did not stipulate full payment for or delivery of the bulbs. Instead, they were futures or forward contracts that "promised" bulb delivery at some point in the future. Many of these contracts were not paid in full; rather, they honored personal credit, which served to increase the level of speculation. The Dutch government played an important role in this, too. It initiated a policy that allowed all parties involved in tulip speculation to purchase an official government certificate for 3.5 percent of the total value of the transaction. The holder of such a certificate could subsequently renege on any contract involving tulips without incurring any penalty. That is, investors could buy a cast-iron insurance policy against any potential losses from tulip speculation for just 3.5 percent of the nominal value of the transaction. This policy bears a striking resemblance to the credit default swap (CDS), which was held largely responsible for causing the 2007–2008 global financial crisis. A typical scenario involved an investor paying a premium to an insurance company in return for a policy that covered their potential losses from investing in toxic assets in the real estate sector.

In order to stabilize the market, the Dutch government also banned all short sale tulip transactions. Without the option of selling short, investors who held negative views of future tulip prices were unable to trade. This did indeed stabilize the falling market over the short term, but it did nothing to prevent the tulip bubble from bursting in the end.

The average price of a tulip bulb increased from a base of 100 to about 1,800 in a matter of months, only to drop back to around 100 over the next couple of years. Interestingly, the speculation was so intense that the tulip bubble started to impact on the prices of other exotic flowers, which experienced similarly volatile fluctuations. Once again, this is consistent with the pattern of most modern bubbles, in which a whole class of assets tends to experience exponential growth before bursting.

The UK railway mania

The first railway line was laid in Britain in 1825, and at the time many people believed that the steam engine would revolutionize the country. Moreover, there was a parallel revolution in the newspaper industry, which led to greater awareness of the possibilities of stock investment in general and regular access to information about the railway companies in particular. And almost all of the newspapers offered the same advice—railway-related stocks and bonds were a sure-fire way to make a fortune. Consequently, there was no shortage of eager investors.

The British government also helped to pump up the railway bubble. Parliament believed that railway construction was not only good for business development but also in the public interest. As a result, the government sanctioned the construction of about 2,700 miles of railway track in 1845—more than the total distance that had been laid in all previous years. Five years later, Britain could boast of 6,000 miles of completed railway lines, with another 1,000 miles under construction (similar to the total length of the country's rail network today).

In contrast to the feverish conglomerate-backed railway investment of the mid-1830s, between 1840 and 1845 the railway bubble was inflated primarily by ordinary British households. Many of them invested their life savings in railway company bonds, most of which promised annualized returns in excess of 10 percent. Meanwhile, many Members of Parliament not only invested in but launched their own railway projects. So it was hardly surprising that Parliament gave the green light to every one of the 272 bills relating to railway construction that were proposed in the mid-nineteenth century.

Eventually, even the promised bond returns of 10 percent proved insufficient to attract new investors, so the railway companies started to issue stocks. As the prices of these stocks continued to rise, ever more capital flowed into the British railway industry, with the total exceeding 100 million pounds between 1843 and 1850. In 1847, the railway industry accounted for 7 percent of Britain's GDP and more than 20 percent of the nation's total domestic investment.

By then, however, the railway bubble had already reached its peak. Towards the end of 1845, the Bank of England raised its interest rate in a bid to curb inflation. Investors who had been anxious to buy more shares only weeks before suddenly scrambled to dump those they already held. During 1846, some railway companies' stock prices rose by 400 percent before subsequently falling by 85 percent before the year was out (which equates to an overall drop of 25 percent over the course of the whole year).

As liquidity tightened and it transpired that many of the proposed projects were infeasible and mired in financial irregularity, more and more railway companies went bust, taking the life savings of thousands of households with them. To make matters worse, many households had also borrowed heavily to boost their investments, which left them deeply indebted and with little hope of breaking even when the bubble burst.

British entrepreneurs and engineers suffered far less than the investors. They turned to overseas markets and built extensive railway networks in Russia, Argentina, China, and the US, among other places.

Unfortunately, investors in the US network made precisely the same mistakes as their British predecessors. Over-building and over-capacity eventually led to a price war among the rival railway companies and deteriorating profit margins. By the end of the nineteenth century, more than a quarter of the US railway industry was bankrupt. This time, though, it was mainly over-optimistic foreign investors who bore the brunt of the losses.

China's warrant bubble

China's warrants contracts in China are very similar to single-name options contracts in the West. They provide investors with the right to exercise when it is in their interests to do so, but impose no obligation to shoulder any losses if the market moves against them.

Commonly used as a hedging tool in the West, warrants contracts became a focus of speculation in China between 2005 and 2007. In China, all securities trade with a T+1 delivery method, with the sole exception of warrants, which trade with a T+0 delivery method. This allows investors to sell any warrants securities that they have bought earlier in the day—a unique arrangement that makes warrants trading ripe for speculation.

At the peak of the speculation, the average daily turnover of warrants trading exceeded 100 percent,[2] meaning that all investors who held warrants in the morning had exited their positions by the afternoon, with the securities bought by new investors.

Why did the investors trade so frenetically? Primarily because they found dumber and/or greedier investors who were willing to pay ever-higher prices for their warrants. This pattern was particularly pronounced near a warrant's expiration date, at which point its value would fall to zero. The daily turnover of such warrants could reach more than 1,000 percent.

This leads us to ask why so many investors were keen to buy securities that would soon be worthless. One possible answer is simple ignorance. Our research revealed that 0.6 percent of all expired warrants were exercised in the wrong way. Upon expiration, some warrants are "in the money," meaning that they should be exercised, whereas others are "out of the money," meaning that they should not be exercised because the investor will lose money if they do so. We found that 0.5 percent of investors "forgot" to exercise their "in the money" options, so they left potential gains on the table. Meanwhile, 0.1 percent of investors chose to exercise "out of the money" options and therefore incurred unnecessary losses.[3] Therefore, as with previous bubbles, it seems that many investors in the Chinese warrants bubble had little understanding of what they were buying.

There is an alternative explanation, however. Many investors were confident that they could always find a fool who would buy their already over-valued warrants at an inflated price. Such speculative logic makes investors utterly oblivious to the fundamentals of their investments. They are interested in nothing but the possibility of ever faster and higher appreciation before the bubble bursts.

Hence, we can say that greed drove the Chinese warrant bubble, as it has every other bubble. As Bernard Baruch said of the Wall Street Crash, "When beggars and shoeshine boys, barbers and beauticians can tell you how to get rich, it is time to remind yourself that there are no more dangerous illusions than the belief that one can get something for nothing." Unfortunately, it is precisely when a bubble approaches its peak that the market reaches unparalleled consensus that speculation is not only safe but offers the most generous returns. When that happens, smart investors would be well advised to think against, rather than with, the crowd and leave the speculation to others.

Real estate bubbles

The Florida real estate bubble of the 1920s

Land is scarce, so it should come as no surprise that real estate is particularly susceptible to speculation and property bubbles.

In the 1920s, the United States gradually became the most important economy in the world. At that time, many people were drawn to the southern state of Florida, attracted by its balmy weather, favorable tax regime, and plenty of undeveloped land. Nevertheless, a large proportion of these migrants were convinced that they had to buy a plot of land as soon as they arrived in case someone swooped in and bought it first. Consequently, land prices in Palm Beach doubled or even tripled over the course of two or three years, and by the middle of the decade a third of Miami's residents were working in real estate and related sectors.[4]

Of course, the boom did not last. The US suffered an economic slowdown from 1926, which in turn had a dramatic impact on property speculation in Florida. Within a year, house prices in many parts of the state had fallen by more than a third. Many households had borrowed heavily to buy their own plots *and* speculated in the booming housing market, so when prices started to fall they lost not only their homes but also their life savings and any access to credit. Interestingly, Florida experienced another real estate boom (and bust) in the first decade of the twenty-first century, with prices in some districts falling by almost 50 percent at the height of the global financial crisis.[5]

Something very similar happened in Hainan, China's largest southern island, in the early 1990s. The tropical beaches, the scarcity of land, and the potential for tourist development combined to attract speculators who watched the market soar and then collapse in the space of a few years.

The Japanese real estate bubble

Regional housing bubbles are not rare, but none can rival the Japanese real estate bubble of the 1980s and 1990s in terms of economic impact.

In 1985, house prices started to rise rapidly throughout Japan. By 1990, on average, a property was worth twice as much as it had been five years earlier. The inflation was even more pronounced in metropolitan areas, with some districts recording 300 percent increases. Moreover, the yen appreciated in the same period, so by 1990 Japan's total land value was estimated at twenty trillion dollars—about 20 percent of the world's total wealth, and twice the size of the total market capitalization of global stock market.[6] Indeed, the land on which the Imperial Palace in central Tokyo is built—a total of 0.75 square miles—was estimated to be worth as much as the whole of California or the whole of Canada. Similarly, at the peak of the bubble, some commercial real estate in Tokyo was valued at 100 million dollars per square meter. Most of these valuations subsequently fell by 90 percent or more over the course of the next decade.

In 1990, almost everyone in Japan took it for granted that house prices were several times higher than those of the US, which had similar GDP per capital. At the same time, unprecedented monetary supply and a real estate development frenzy convinced many Japanese citizens that real estate was the best investment option for them, even though few could really afford to purchase and live in such expensive properties.

With the Plaza Accord and consequent appreciation of the yen, international capital started to withdraw from Japan and the real estate bubble burst. House prices in major metropolitan areas fell by between 70 and 90 percent from their peak values. This huge devaluation resulted in over 600 billion yen's worth of non-performing loans on Japanese banks' balance sheets, the infamous "balance sheet recession," and the so-called "lost decades" of the Japanese economy. Even now, Japan has not fully recovered from the consequences of its real estate bubble, and many Japanese rank it as almost as disastrous for the country as World War II.[7]

Why property bubbles never last

Scarcity of land has been an issue throughout human history. However, developments in information technology and e-commerce mean that geographical proximity is less important than it once was, so households are now less constrained by land scarcity in key metropolitan areas.

The citizens of Amsterdam have been monitoring the city's house price fluctuations for centuries, and these records now serve as a telling example for potential investors. House prices in central Amsterdam, which was one of the most important cities in Western Europe and a global financial center long into the nineteenth century, have increased by 2.3 percent per annum over the past three centuries. That is no different from the Netherlands' average inflation rate over the same period.[8] Similarly, Robert Shiller has shown that US real estate returns are roughly equivalent to inflation over the long term.[9]

The skyscraper effect

China now leads the world in the construction of skyscrapers, which are typically defined as buildings over 500 feet (152 meters) in height. By 2011, it could claim six of the ten tallest buildings in the world, with the skylines of Beijing, Taipei, Shanghai, Hong Kong, Nanjing, and Guangzhou all dominated by impressive towers.[10] In 1990, North America possessed 80 percent of the world's tallest buildings; by 2012, this had fallen to just 18 percent. In the same year, of the 100 tallest buildings in the world, 45 were in Asia, and 34 of them were in China. In total, the country now has more than 800 skyscrapers, four times as many as the United States.

Of course, this skyscraper mania has been propelled by China's unprecedented economic growth over the last two decades and its large, young, increasingly urban population. However, it reminds many commentators of the "skyscraper curse"— a theory proposed by the German analyst Andrew Lawrence which links the completion of prestigious skyscrapers to the start of financial crises. According to Lawrence, "even though the completion of skyscrapers can reflect economic development, it also reflects over-heatedness in an economy and presages crisis."[11] Many examples since the 1920s support his theory: the Empire State Building and the Chrysler Building in New York were completed just before the onset of the Great Depression; the Sears Tower in Chicago and the World Trade Center in New York coincided with the 1970s oil crisis; the Petronas Building in Kuala Lumpur, Malaysia, the Jinmao Building in Shanghai, and Taipei 101 in Taipei all heralded the 1997 Southeast Asian financial crisis; and the Burj Khalifa Tower in Dubai was still being built when the world entered the global financial crisis of 2008.[12]

With China planning to build ever more skyscrapers over the next few years,[13] it remains to be seen whether it will manage to break the skyscrapers' curse.[14] Andrew Lawrence, for one, is not hopeful. He believes that all of the classic ingredients are in place—over-optimistic developers, political aspiration for landmark buildings, and easy lending—so China will probably not escape the curse.

Lessons from history

What can we learn from history? Bubbles have occurred at different times, in different places, when different technology was available, and different financial systems were in place. However, they can all be traced back to one fundamental cause: human beings' inherent greed and fear. This is why it is so important to study human history as well as financial history, because human behavior and decision making evolve at a far slower pace than technology and financial innovations. Moreover, understanding human history helps us understand our place in that history, and allows us to assess the wisdom of following the crowd, especially when that crowd is in a frenzy. In addition, every government should study history in order to understand the long-term trends in economic development. With luck, this will persuade the world's politicians to abandon their attempts to shore up global economic growth through short-term stimulus, a policy that may have disastrous long-term consequences.

Similarly, investors who are living through a bubble must ask themselves whether the party will really last for ever. If history tells us anything, it is that the greater the short-term returns, the less likely they are to continue for any length of time. However, greed and fear, along with selective amnesia, have caused generation after generation of investors to repeat the same obvious mistakes over and over again.

As we have seen, on average, the US stock market enjoyed annual returns of 11–12 percent over the course of the last century. Hence, if returns are significantly higher than this average for any length of time (such as during the great bull market of the 1990s), then there is a strong possibility that the subsequent period will suffer disappointing performance (as happened between 2000 and 2009). Statisticians term this simple concept "regression towards the mean," and neither wishful thinking nor fear has any effect on it. However, under the powerful influence of their behavioral biases, most people find it almost impossible to accept the inevitability of regression towards the mean.

In 2011, Carmen M. Reinhart and Kenneth S. Rogoff published *This Time is Different*, in which they reflected on the many follies of human financial history.[15] In particular, they emphasized that generation after generation have fallen into the same trap of believing that the traditional rules and laws no longer apply. Yet history tells us that old habits die hard, and human nature has remained unchanged for millennia.

China's economy and financial system have been going through an unprecedented transformation since the 1980s. Although the rapid pace of development has been widely applauded, there are worrying signs that China is repeating the mistakes of earlier financial superpowers and may face increasing risks and challenges as a result. The country's leaders need to learn from history, so at this point it may be useful to provide a summary of the key elements that contribute to the development of most bubbles.

Technological and financial innovations

A new idea, concept, or technology always seems to lie at the heart of every bubble. These novel developments stimulate people's hopes and speculation, and lead them to question the validity of traditional wisdom and investment principles. Their very novelty makes them mysterious and difficult to understand and price, resulting in further speculation and the so-called "self-fulfilling" prophecy—speculation pushes up asset prices, which generates further speculation.

Financial innovations have also served as catalysts for a number of bubbles. For example, the "portfolio insurance" strategy was blamed for the 1987 stock market bubble and crash; the rapid development of online trading certainly contributed to the 1998–2000 internet bubble; and CDSs and collateralized debt obligations

(CDOs) were important factors in the 2008 global financial crisis. Moreover, because financial innovations and business model innovations are harder to assess than technological innovations, some commentators argue that they are more important in the creation of bubbles.

Excessive liquidity

Excessive liquidity has been a key element in every bubble. This is because it suppresses the yield on risk-free assets, forcing investors to chase ever-riskier investment options that promise higher returns. Investors who fall into this trap abandon their investment discipline and ignore the market forces that eventually cause a bubble to develop. Moreover, the greater the liquidity, the bigger the bubble.

Investor irrationality and lack of sophistication

The scale of the bubble is also related to the experience and sophistication of investors. Laboratory research into bubble formation has found that large bubbles develop when subjects participate in the experiment for the first time. However, when subjects are invited to participate again, the bubble peaks much earlier and never grows as large. Even more tellingly, no bubble forms when subjects participate for a third time.[16]

The implications of such findings are obvious: if one has prior experience of a bubble, one is likely to reject the opportunity to buy assets near the next bubble's peak. Such mass avoidance will limit the growth of most bubbles. Moreover, any inexperienced investors who are tempted to buy assets as the bubble grows will observe how their more experienced counterparts are behaving and rein in their own speculation. This combination of self-control among experienced investors and rational herding behavior among inexperienced investors will usually burst the bubble before it grows too large.

One empirical US study found that investors with prior experience of stock market crashes (such as the Wall Street Crash) tend to take fewer risks later in life and rarely participate in subsequent bubbles. However, consistent with our earlier discussion about investor behavior, the researchers found that this aversion to speculation gradually diminishes over time.[17]

This phenomenon explains why investor composition has such a significant impact on the riskiness and stability of markets. Bubbles form most frequently in relatively new markets in developing economies because they tend to contain high proportions of young, inexperienced investors. Hence, over recent decades, numerous bubbles have formed in Asia's financial markets.[18]

Government support

Either explicit or implicit government support has contributed to every major bubble since the days of tulip mania. Governments have promoted excessive liquidity, provided rash guarantees to investors, and even used their privileged positions to profit from speculation, often with the justification that they are stimulating economic growth. But their actions merely push asset prices to unsustainable heights and generate one bubble after another. Many analysts were surprised when Japan's extremely loose monetary policy and quantitative easing failed to lift the country out of its economic malaise after two decades of stagnation. But if they had read their history they would have known that crises are rarely solved—in fact they tend to deepen—when governments try to boost growth and iron out kinks in the economic cycle.

To make matters worse, the continuous government intervention and liquidity injection that have propped up the global economic and financial system over recent decades have made it hard to envisage a return to the old days, when market forces generated organic, sustainable growth in the world economy.

Notes

1 Schama, S. 1997. *The Embarrassment of Riches*. New York: Vintage.
2 Liao, L., Li, Z., Zhang, W., and Zhu, N. 2010. *Security Supply and the Bubble: A Natural Experiment from the Chinese Warrants Market*. Working paper, Shanghai Advanced Institute of Finance.
3 Liao, L., Li, Z., Zhang, W., and Zhu, N. 2010. *Security Supply and the Bubble: A Natural Experiment from the Chinese Warrants Market*. Working paper, Shanghai Advanced Institute of Finance.
4 www.library.hbs.edu/hc/crises/forgotten.html.
5 www.thebubblebubble.com/florida-property-bubble/.
6 http://en.wikipedia.org/wiki/Japanese_asset_price_bubble.
7 www.businessinsider.com/richard-koo-the-world-in-balance-sheet-recession-2012-4?op=1.
8 Eichholtz, P. 1999. A Long Run House Index: The Herengratch Index 1628–1973. *Real Estate Economics*, 25: 175–192.
9 www.theglobeandmail.com/globe-investor/personal-finance/mortgages/will-inflation-keep-boosting-house-prices-dont-bet-on-it/article4792362/.
10 http://fdc.soufun.com/news/2012-01-03/6767370_1.html.
11 www.economist.com/news/finance-and-economics/21647289-there-such-thing-skyscraper-curse-towers-babel.
12 http://news.ifeng.com/gundong/detail_2011_09/19/9294611_0.shtml?_from_ralated.
13 http://news.ifeng.com/mainland/detail_2011_09/19/9297802_0.shtml.
14 http://news.ifeng.com/gundong/detail_2011_09/19/9294611_0.shtml?_from_ralated.
15 Reinhart, C.M. and Rogoff, K.S. 2011. *This Time is Different*. Princeton, NJ: Princeton University Press.
16 Liao, L., Li, Z., Zhang, W., and Zhu, N. 2010. *Security Supply and the Bubble: A Natural Experiment from the Chinese Warrants Market*. Working paper, Shanghai Advanced Institute of Finance.
17 Malmendier, U. and Nagel, S. 2011. Depression Babies: Do Macroeconomic Experiences Affect Risk-Taking? *Quarterly Journal of Economics*, 126(1): 373–416.
18 Chang, M.C., Tsai, C.-L., Wu, R.C.-F., and Zhu, N. 2013. *Sentiment, Market Order Choice, and Returns*. Working paper, Shanghai Advanced Institute of Finance.

9
LEARNING BY INVESTING

Given the various behavioral biases that blight investors' judgment, it is natural to ask why they find it so hard to recognize and overcome them. Part of the answer lies in the fact that investment is one of the most difficult areas to study. Effective learning is facilitated by immediate, clear, and repeated feedback. For example, Pavlov rang a bell whenever he provided food for the canine subjects of his experiment, and the dogs gradually learned to associate the bell with the food. If specific actions lead to certain outcomes time and time again, the consequences of one's decisions become obvious and one learns to adjust one's behavior accordingly.

Unfortunately, people who invest in securities have few opportunities to learn in this simple, cause-and-effect way. First of all, many of them trade infrequently and do not have a set holding period. This means that their selling decisions usually depend heavily on their investment performance. As we have seen, if their investments lose money, they tend to hold on to the losing stocks in the hope that they will bounce back and at least break even. Investors who behave in this way usually have little understanding of the performance of their investments. Many do not acknowledge the loss because it is only "on paper" until the stocks are actually sold, so they delay that sale for as long as possible, losing ever more money in the process.

Second, global macro-economic conditions, domestic industrial policy, regional development projects, and firm-specific information all affect investment performance, so investors are bombarded with complex and often contradictory information that they should consider. However, faced with this avalanche of information, many investors abandon any attempt to analyze it properly and instead base their investment decisions on simple but flawed heuristics, such as a stock's previous performance.

Third, investors tend to lose interest in their investments over time. This is particularly true of falling stocks, which some investors deliberately ignore because of the so-called "ostrich effect." Any investor who behaves in this way will find it impossible to develop an unbiased and reliable perception of her own ability.

Fourth, it can be difficult to assess the wisdom of a particular investment decision. Most retail investors keep it very simple: they are happy whenever they make money and disappointed whenever they lose money. But focusing on absolute returns in this way does not a give true picture of the investor's performance because it ignores important considerations, such as overall market performance and level of portfolio risk.

Unsurprisingly, most retail investors feel great about their investments during bull markets, and miserable during bear markets. Clearly, then, the absolute returns of their portfolios are of paramount importance when they come to evaluate their investment ability. Yet retail investors' returns relative to the market benchmark tend to *improve* during bear markets. In other words, they perform better than average when the market falls, and worse than average when the market rises. This is because over-exuberance causes investors to make irrational decisions and forgo valuable investment opportunities during bull markets.

Investors need to learn the true opportunity costs of their investments. They already know that passive investment in an index fund or an exchange-traded fund will guarantee at least average market returns, so they should always measure their performance against the market index, rather than merely calculate their absolute returns. Only then will they gain an accurate picture of their investing ability.

Furthermore, many investors focus on a small proportion of their stocks—those that have made profits—rather than the whole portfolio when evaluating their investing abilities. Of course, this results in over-confidence and a false sense of accomplishment. A majority of retail investors will happily brag about their winning trades and never mention the stocks that have dropped like stones when discussing their "knack for investment" with friends and colleagues.

Most investors also fail to take risk into account when evaluating their investment abilities. Some get lucky by investing in risky stocks at the start of a bull market, make substantial returns, and interpret this as indicative of their superior investment ability. However, such over-confidence causes them to ignore their limitations, increase their risk-taking, and ultimately suffer significant losses when their luck turns. Those who refuse to acknowledge their initial good fortune exhibit unjustifiable faith in their own ability and speculate wildly during feverish market conditions, then become increasingly desperate during market corrections. Consequently, many retail investors enter the market just as it peaks, then cash in their over-priced stocks just as it bottoms out.

Given that learning about investment is a slow, vague, and intermittent process, most retail investors—even those who have traded for decades—fail to develop an accurate picture of their investment ability. That is unfortunate, because it is impossible to assess one's optimal risk tolerance or devise effective investment strategies without a clear understanding of one's ability. To make matters even worse, psychological researchers have found that people's (over-)confidence *increases* when they face difficult, unfamiliar tasks. Of course, this leads to more rash mistakes than one might expect.[1] As an ancient Chinese proverb says, "He who has no knowledge has no fear."

Admittedly, recent advances in information technology have given investors unprecedented opportunities to explore information and improve their investment ability. However, too much information—information overload—may result in over-confidence and a false sense of control, which in turn may impair investors' learning. Researchers have found that gamblers who are given access to abundant information about horses and jockeys develop greater confidence in their bets than those who are provided with less information. However, crucially, those in the well-informed group make no more money than the ignorant gamblers. In fact, the accuracy of their predictions declines as their information increases. Something similar seems to happen during bull markets, when investors often treat every piece of gossip they hear as accurate information.[2]

As we saw earlier in the book, investors also tend to prefer companies that are based in their home city, region, or country. Once again, this suggests that any sort of information (irrespective of whether it indicates a company's stock is likely to grow) can foster unjustified confidence and lead to sub-optimal investment decisions.[3] Investors who are unduly confident in their own ability are likely to make hasty decisions whenever they hear a snippet of information, negating any potential advantage the information may have provided.[4] Therefore, rival investors with no access to information are not necessarily at a disadvantage. Indeed, their relative ignorance may prompt them to exercise more vigilance and careful consideration about their investments.[5]

In summary, learning how to invest wisely is a very difficult process. Nevertheless, investors can learn how to improve their performance over time, as behavioral finance research has proved. This learning may be either passive or active.

Passive learning is easy to understand. Say an investor opens an investment account with 10,000 dollars and loses 30 percent during his first year of trading, another 30 percent during his second year of trading, and yet another 30 percent during his third year of trading. Consequently, after three years of stock market speculation, he has lost almost all of his original capital. By now, he has probably learned that his investment ability is not that great.

Active learning refers to investors who actively adjust their investment decisions on the basis of their own assessments of their investment abilities. Specifically, a rational learner should increase both her risk-taking and the amount of money she has invested when she believes that she has a talent for investment, and decrease her risk-taking and level of investment when she believes that she lacks investment ability.

We conducted an empirical study which found some evidence of such active learning, mostly among investors who increased their risk-taking after making a good investment. However, this could be due to self-attribution—a manifestation of over-confidence—as such investors may credit themselves with making wise investment decisions while ignoring factors such as risk and good fortune. In contrast, we found little evidence of investors reducing their risk-taking or level of investment after losing money. Again, this is consistent with self-attribution, as people tend to blame bad outcomes on other factors rather than their own poor decision making. Such asymmetrical interpretation of one's own investment performance hinders effective learning about one's true investment ability and does little to improve one's future investment decisions.[6]

Furthermore, investors do not learn from and adjust their investment decisions in a timely fashion. In much of our research we have noticed that reactions to making money (in the form of adjusting one's position) are almost immediate, but there is no similarly rapid response to losing money. That is, investors take much longer to adjust their positions after their stocks fall. This helps to explain why it may be several years before an investor realizes that her investment ability is poor.[7]

Third, new investors are investing additional capital in the stock market every year. As a result, less experienced investors are always entering the market. This phenomenon is particularly pronounced in Asia, where the markets themselves and the investors are both relatively young. Investors in such dynamic markets find it especially difficult to assess their ability because there is a shortage of reliable and consistent benchmarks against which to measure their performance.[8]

Learning about investing is also hindered by the way in which most people's minds work. Human beings' natural tendency is to remember their greatest achievements, but to forget about the effort that led to them.[9] People also vividly remember their own episodes of public embarrassment for a long time, yet quickly forget about such incidents when they witness them happening to someone else.[10]

In sports that are scored subjectively (such as gymnastics, diving, and trampolining), most competitors prefer slots at the beginning or end of the event, rather than in the middle. Psychological research has provided an explanation for this: people tend to remember the first and last choices in a sequence, rather than those that appear in the middle.[11]

The limitations of people's memories are evident in the legal world, too. Witnesses often have trouble remembering a crime scene accurately even shortly after the crime has taken place. They tend to recall anything that is out of the ordinary, but have little recollection of other crucial but mundane details. In addition, eyewitnesses have little trouble identifying suspects from their own ethnic group, but routinely fail to identify suspects belonging to other ethnic groups.[12]

All of this suggests that people find it hard to employ scientific methodology—such as probability theory or the law of large numbers—even when dealing with relatively simple matters. It may also explain why investors find it so difficult to assess their own performance and reach an accurate conclusion about their investment ability. In laboratory experiments, many subjects have a hard time remembering what happened just one year ago, let alone three years ago, or a decade ago. This probably goes some way to explaining why financial markets experience booms and busts every few years, as if the previous crashes have never happened.[13]

Notes

1 Russo, J.E. and Schoemaker, P.J.H. 1989. *Decision Traps*. New York: Doubleday.
2 Oskamp, S. 1965. Overconfidence in Case-Study Judgments. *Journal of Consulting Psychology*, 29(3): 261–265; Fischhoff, B., Slovic, P., and Lichtenstein, S. 1977. Knowing with Certainty: The Appropriateness of Extreme Confidence. *Journal of Experimental Psychology: Human Perception and Performance*, 3(4): 552–564.
3 Zhu, N. 2003. *The Local Bias of Individual Investors*. Working paper, Yale University.
4 Seasholes, M.S. and Zhu, N. 2010. Individual Investors and Local Bias. *Journal of Finance*, 65(5): 1987–2010.
5 Li, L., Liao, Z., Zhang, W., and Zhu, N. 2012. Does the Location of Stock Exchange Matter? A Within-Country Analysis. *Pacific-Basin Finance Journal*, 20(4): 561–582.
6 Adams, P.A. and Adams, J.K. 1960. Confidence in the Recognition and Reproduction of Words Difficult to Spell. *American Journal of Psychology*, 73(4): 544–552; Ross, M. and Sicoly, F. 1979. Egocentric Biases in Availability and Attribution. *Journal of Personality and Social Psychology*, 37: 322–336; Shepperd, J., Malone, W., and Sweeny, K. 2008. Exploring Causes of the Self-Serving Bias. *Social and Personality Psychology Compass*, 2(2): 895–908.
7 Nicolosi, G., Peng, L., and Zhu, N. 2009. Do Individual Investors Learn from Their Trading Experience? *Journal of Financial Markets*, 12(2): 317–366; Seru, A., Shumway, T., and Stoffman, N. 2009. Learning by Trading. *Review of Financial Studies*, 23(2): 705–739.
8 Chang, M.C., Tsai, C.L., Wu, C.F., and Zhu, N. 2012. *Market Sentiment and Market Order Choice*. Working paper, Shanghai Advanced Institute of Finance.
9 Mitchell, T. and Thompson, L. 1994. A Theory of Temporal Adjustments of the Evaluation of Events: Rosy Prospection and Rosy Retrospection. In Stubbart, C., Porac, J., and Meindl, J. (eds.), *Advances in Managerial Cognition and Organizational Information-Processing*. Greenwich, CT: JAI Press.
10 Mitchell, T. and Thompson, L. 1994. A Theory of Temporal Adjustments of the Evaluation of Events: Rosy Prospection and Rosy Retrospection. In Stubbart, C., Porac, J., and Meindl, J. (eds.), *Advances in Managerial Cognition and Organizational Information-Processing*. Greenwich, CT: JAI Press; Von Restorff, H. 1933. Über die Wirkung von Bereichsbildungen im Spurenfeld. *Psychological Research*, 18(1): 299–342.
11 Mather, M. and Johnson, M.K. (2000). Choice-Supportive Source Monitoring: Do Our Decisions Seem Better to Us as We Age? *Psychology and Aging*, 15: 596–606; http://duncanpierce.org/cognitive_bias_workshop.
12 Hess, U., Kappas, A., and Bause, R. 1995. The Intensity of Facial Expression is Determined by Underlying Affective States and Social Situations. *Journal of Personality and Social Psychology*, 69(2): 280–288; Elfenbein, H.A. and Ambady, N. 2003. When Familiarity Breeds Accuracy: Cultural Exposure and Facial Emotion Recognition. *Journal of Personality and Social Psychology*, 85(2): 276–290.
13 http://www.time.com/time/health/article/0,8599,1817329,00.html; http://neurosciencenews.com/remembering-to-forget-autobiographical-memories-ptsd-negative-emotions/.

10
OVER-CONFIDENT CEOs

This chapter deals primarily with the behavioral biases of corporate executives. Granted, executives are the best of the best in the corporate world. Almost all of the world's CEOs can point to some extraordinary achievements that have helped them reach their current status. These impressive track records and accomplishments tend to induce considerable confidence among CEOs. This should come as no surprise, as corporate boards and head hunters often list confidence as a crucial executive attribute. CEOs are expected to display total confidence in their strategic plans, leadership, and execution, and then lead their teams to new heights.[1]

Unfortunately, however, researchers at the University of California found that many CEOs are a bit *too* confident.[2] They looked at star CEOs—those who had won prestigious awards (such as *Business Week*'s "CEO of the Year"), media stars (such as Oprah Winfrey and Martha Stewart), and genuine pioneers (such as Bill Gates and Mark Zuckerberg)—and compared their management activities with a control sample of CEOs who had so far failed to attain celebrity status.

They found that the star CEOs were more likely to:

1. publish their memoirs and other books;[3]
2. serve on the boards of other companies;
3. engage in earnings management so that their company earnings meet or exceed Wall Street's forecasts; and
4. play off a lower handicap in golf.

In other words, star CEOs spend less time in hands-on management of their corporations once they have attained their star status. Indeed, they are more likely to engage in the acquisition of other businesses rather than focus on running their own.

In a separate study, the same researchers found that star CEOs, along with other CEOs who hold a large number of company stocks (another indication of a CEO's confidence in his or her own business), are 65 percent more likely to acquire other companies than CEOs from the control group.[4] That is interesting enough in itself, but the researchers were more interested in how those acquisitions subsequently performed. When compared with the companies run by CEOs from the control group, those managed by over-confident CEOs under-performed by 15–26 percent over the next three years. Moreover, in addition to their poor stock market performance, they fared badly in terms of operational and financial efficiency. Key indicators such as return on assets, return on equities, return on invested capital, and earnings growth were all 10–15 percent worse than those of the control companies. And yet, despite their disappointing performance, the over-confident CEOs enjoyed far larger compensation packages than the control CEOs, largely because the star CEOs received a greater proportion of their total compensation in the form of stock options.

So, why do star CEOs generate such poor results?

One somewhat surprising explanation is that the announcement of any acquisition typically has an immediate negative impact on the acquirer's stock price. Moreover, the shares in the acquiring firm usually continue to lag behind those of control companies over the next couple of years.[5] Even more interestingly, the market seems to be especially averse to acquisitions that are initiated by celebrity CEOs. Such transactions typically cause the acquiring firm's stock price to fall by 0.9 percent over the three-day announcement window, whereas acquisitions that are initiated by control group CEOs do not have such a pronounced negative effect. Furthermore, acquirers who finance their transactions with stock swaps suffer 1.35 percent falls within the three-day announcement window, whereas acquirers who finance their transactions with cash typically *gain* 0.5 percent within the announcement window.

So, why does the market punish star CEOs who finance their acquisitions with stock swaps? The answer draws us back to the problem of over-confidence.

Most companies engage in acquisitions in pursuit of synergy. For companies with little internal growth potential, external acquisition may be the fastest and easiest way for them to expand. Instead of returning profits to investors, many corporate executives advocate growth through acquisition with the justification that larger companies enjoy greater influence. And, of course, there is the incidental benefit that larger firms tend to reward their senior executives with more lucrative compensation packages. Moreover, executives usually experience greater job satisfaction when they manage a larger company.

The market's overwhelming negativity towards acquisitions initiated by over-confident CEOs may reflect investors' suspicion that such CEOs often over-estimate the benefits of synergy and under-estimate the costs of acquisition. Indeed, precisely because of their past successes, over-confident CEOs have a tendency to pay over the odds for their acquisition targets, and therefore increase both the cost and the risk of such transactions. Consequently, whenever a star CEO pays too much for a target, there is an inevitable transfer of wealth from the acquiring company's to the target company's shareholders.[6]

The reason why the market prefers cash-financed to stock-financed acquisitions is a little more complicated. First of all, any company that engages in the former type of acquisition must have ample cash, which usually indicates rock-solid performance and financial stability. Second, the market will always draw its own conclusions on the basis of the firm's choice of financing. If the acquiring company decides to pay cash for the target company, the conclusion is simple: the acquiring company believes that the target company is worth more than it has offered.

However, everything becomes much more complicated when the acquiring CEO tries to fund the acquisition with shares in his or her own company. Sometimes, a company will make an offer for another business not because it feels that the target company is a particularly cheap or attractive proposition, but because the acquiring company itself feels that it has been over-valued by the market. Although this is not the motivation behind all stock-financed acquisitions, the fact that it *could be* certainly has an impact on market opinion.

As we saw earlier, Mark Cuban, the founder of Broadcast.com, sold his company to Yahoo for 5.9 billion dollars' worth of Yahoo shares. He did not wait long before selling the stock at 163 dollars per share—a valuation that Yahoo has not approached since the internet bubble burst soon afterwards (at the time of writing, in 2016, they were trading at 41 dollars per share). Cuban told his colleagues that his own company was worth nothing like 5.9 billion dollars, and that Yahoo's stock was also seriously over-valued, but most of them ignored him, held on to their Yahoo shares, and lost fortunes as a result. Similar incidents happen all the time, especially when the market is booming, which helps to explain why professional investors (especially those with good memories) are so skeptical about stock-financed acquisitions.

Will SOE acquisition continue to drive Chinese economic growth?

Over 100 Chinese businesses were ranked in the Fortune 500 list of the world's largest companies in 2015, more than twice as many as had appeared in the same list a decade earlier. Most of these Chinese companies could be distinguished from their international counterparts for two reasons. First, almost all of them were state-owned enterprises (SOEs). Second, although many of them suffered operating losses in 2015, both their revenues and their size had increased dramatically, partly because of a series of blockbuster mergers and acquisitions.

The presence of so many Chinese firms among the elite of the corporate world has led to applause and concern in almost equal measure. As the pace of Chinese economic growth continues to slow, ever more commentators are starting to ask what will drive the country's growth in the future. While most people agree that the government must let the market play a greater role in setting key factor prices and interest rates, there has been considerable debate over which type of enterprise—state-owned or privately owned—will be more instrumental in helping China adapt its economic growth model and sustain the economic miracle of the past two decades.

A casual assessment would suggest that SOEs have clear advantages over private firms. First of all, at present, all of China's largest companies—measured by total assets and total market capitalization—are SOEs, and several of these now rank among the largest companies in the world. Second, some SOEs enjoy either monopolistic or oligopolistic power in their sectors, and there is no sign of any significant competition emerging in the near future. Furthermore, on the back of their strong market power, some SOEs have expanded beyond their traditional areas of operation and into more lucrative sectors, such as real estate development and financial services.

However, the situation is more complicated than it seems at first glance. First, given that most SOEs have quite complex objectives, few manage to develop any sort of expertise in profit-making, and Chinese SOEs are no exception. Although the days when the Chinese railway system had its own police force are long gone, many SOEs still run their own hospitals, middle schools, restaurants, and catering businesses. All SOEs are expected to do more than generate the best returns for their shareholders, so their managers invariably have to juggle multiple and often conflicting objectives at the same time. Given that profit maximization is not the sole—or even the principal—criterion by which SOEs are evaluated, it is difficult to estimate the extent to which they will be able to contribute to Chinese economic growth in the future.

Moreover, the vast majority of the senior managers in Chinese SOEs are also members of the Chinese civil service, and most of them harbor political rather than commercial ambitions. As a result, they are more interested in company size than profits, and focus on the speed of growth rather than the quality. This is reflected in the fact that almost all of the largest profit losers in the Chinese A-share market are SOEs or subsidiaries of SOEs.

Another important factor to consider is the quality of corporate governance within most Chinese SOEs. Because the state is the dominant shareholder in every SOE, all other shareholders lack the power or indeed the incentive to monitor the company and its senior management team. This lack of scrutiny can lead to serious problems, such as corporate empire building, excessive executive compensation packages and perquisites, tunneling, and even fraud and stock market manipulation. Furthermore, SOEs have suffered some of the largest trading losses in Chinese corporate history, such as those at China Aviation Oil and CITIC Pacific. These incidents highlight the importance of balancing various stakeholders within SOEs, and suggest that such enterprises are not particularly good at enforcing internal checks and balances.

Partly for these reasons, if one were to look beyond China's borders, one would see that the trend over the past decade has been towards ever more SOE privatization. By facilitating the introduction of private capital into SOEs, many developed and developing economies, including Great Britain, Japan, and India, have witnessed some of their largest SOE companies reap the benefits of increased market influence.

It seems inevitable that SOEs will eventually face similar challenges to those that the Soviet Union faced just prior to its collapse. The principle of the "invisible hand" decrees that market forces can provide enough incentives to find out information, which is critical in allocating resources efficiently. However, centrally planned economies and SOEs lack such incentives in information collecting, which results in poor decision making and tremendous investment losses as a result. Even if the SOEs are able to provide some much-needed short-term impetus to the Chinese economy, the trillion-dollar question is whether they will be able to sustain that contribution? And if they cannot, how should they be reformed?

COFCO: a case study

Many Chinese SOEs, especially those that fall under the auspices of the State-Owned Asset Supervision and Administration Commission (SASAC), have engaged in a series of aggressive mergers and acquisitions over the past decade. COFCO is one of them.[7]

After starting life as a specialist foreign trading company in the grain and oil sector, COFCO gradually transformed itself into a food and beverage conglomerate that spanned production, processing, and trade. By acquiring a large number of companies in related industries, its revenues increased considerably while its lines of business multiplied exponentially.[8] However, when one examines each of those lines of business individually, a very different picture starts to emerge. Out of the seven listed companies that made up COFCO in 2012, five suffered considerable losses in that year. Only COFCO packaging and COFCO real estate made profits. In particular, COFCO TunHe suffered losses of 700 million yuan, even though its revenues rose at double-digit pace.

COFCO is not an unusual case among Chinese SOEs. SASAC uses a range of diverse criteria when evaluating their success or failure. This may be part of the reason why Chinese companies, and especially SOEs, are serial acquirers and so keen to expand their lines of business: in theory, this sort of growth should generate greater market power and higher profits for the enterprise. However, as the COFCO case reveals, integrating many different lines of business, as well as upper-stream and lower-stream elements from a single line of business, does not necessarily guarantee success for the subsidiary companies or indeed the enterprise as a whole. Any potential efficiency gains may be lost due to coordination issues as the business becomes ever more complex. Moreover, because SOE decision making is opaque and not subjected to the capital market's short-term oversight and judgment, it is often a long time before an accurate assessment of the wisdom of merger and acquisition transactions may be made. For example, COFCO suffered serious losses after deciding to enter the wine industry, and ultimately had to admit that it had got its timing badly wrong.[9]

Many Chinese SOEs are attracted by the idea of acquiring upstream raw materials, under the assumption that raw materials are rare, so gaining control over their production and supply is a sure-fire way to establish and maintain profitability throughout the whole value chain. However, most raw materials can now be acquired quite simply in the secondary securities market, and indeed hedged against future price fluctuations in the futures market. Buying raw materials on the open market not only provides companies with greater flexibility, but also saves them the trouble of managing the upstream enterprises that supply them, which can be both costly and risky.

Furthermore, every business empire becomes more complex as it grows, which makes effective communication and decision making increasingly challenging. For example, there has been little business-line collaboration among COFCO's plants in NingXia, XinJiang, and Tianjin.

It is quite possible that some unforeseen benefits of the Chinese SOEs' frenetic merger and acquisition activity will eventually emerge. However, it is equally likely that some of China's largest companies are simply repeating the mistakes that were made by Japan's conglomerates during that country's economic bubble period. Numerous Japanese companies made big splashes in the first year after their acquisition, then the deals started to lose their luster in the second year, and finally the companies failed miserably during the third year.

Notes

1 www.ceo.com/media_type/ceo_guides/guide_leadership/how-great-leaders-get-great-confidence/; http://blogs.hbr.org/cs/2012/07/less_confident_people_are_more_su.html.
2 Malmendier, U. and Tate, G. 2005. CEO Overconfidence and Corporate Investment. *Journal of Finance*, 60(6): 2661–2700.
3 Malmendier, U. and Tate, G. 2009. Superstar CEOs. *Quarterly Journal of Economics*, 124(4): 1593–1638.
4 Malmendier, U. and Tate, G. 2008. Who Makes Acquisitions? CEO Overconfidence and the Market's Reaction. *Journal of Financial Economics*, 89(1): 20–43.
5 Malmendier, U. and Tate, G. 2008. Who Makes Acquisitions? CEO Overconfidence and the Market's Reaction. *Journal of Financial Economics*, 89(1): 20–43.
6 Thaler, R.H. 1988. Anomalies: The Winner's Curse. *Journal of Economic Perspectives*, 2(1): 191–202.
7 http://money.163.com/11/1012/09/7G5H5Q2L00253B0H.html.
8 www.ce.cn/cysc/sp/subject/2009/mn/.
9 http://finance.sina.com.cn/roll/20110225/20199435585.shtml.

11
CATERING CEOs

While corporate executives suffer from the usual behavioral biases, they enjoy many advantages over regular investors in terms of their access to company information and familiarity with the way in which the capital markets operate. Indeed, many executives take advantage of retail investors' lack of understanding of certain corporate activities to create wealth and/or boost share prices without doing much to improve actual company performance.

IPO financing

An initial public offering (IPO) marks the first occasion when a company's shares are traded on a public market. The subscriptions to and pricing of a major IPO not only determine the amount of capital raised for the company but also serve as important benchmarks for the pricing of similar transactions in the future.

The main aim of the IPO process is to determine the price at which a company's shares should be offered to investors in a securities market. In this sense, IPO investors are not too different from purchasers of fruit and vegetables at a market. If the listing firm deliberately prices its shares towards the high end of its valuation, the company clearly wants to keep more for itself and offer less to investors, and vice versa. However, one peculiar aspect of the IPO process is that investors often display a stronger appetite for IPO shares when the pricing is high. Of course, this runs contrary to economic theory, which states that lower prices stimulate demand.[1]

Investors' somewhat bizarre preference for high-priced shares is largely due to the timing of IPOs. Private companies can secure financing through the equities market (IPO or seasoned equity offering (SEO)) or through the fixed income market (corporate bond). Naturally, each company will choose the most attractive and economical option for itself—namely, whichever method is likely to generate the largest amount of capital for the lowest financing cost. As a result, one often finds a cluster of IPOs during "hot" market conditions, when stock valuations are high. During less attractive market conditions, more companies choose to issue bonds or abandon their financing attempts altogether. There are numerous examples of companies canceling their planned IPOs because market conditions were unfavorable and insufficient financing would be secured as a result.[2]

In the United States, IPO deals spiked in 1929, 1974, and 1999, three peak market periods, reflecting the fact that companies have historically timed their IPOs to coincide with a buoyant market when shares tend to be over-valued. Of course, this places potential investors in something of a dilemma: they may suspect that the asking price for a company's shares is too high, but they know that they will have only one chance to invest in that company's IPO. Unfortunately, many retail investors go ahead and buy the shares anyway, and then they fall in price, leaving investors with losses rather than profits. This pattern is repeated around the world, with IPO stocks significantly under-performing shares in comparable companies that have been listed on the market for some time. The same is true of SEO shares.[3]

Another reason why IPO shares can be sold at a premium is because so many interested parties—corporate founders, early stage venture capitalists, cornerstone investors, and private equity investors—are attracted by the offerings, so competition for the shares can be fierce. Moreover, it is not uncommon for pre-IPO companies to make over-optimistic forecasts about their growth potential, or to employ earnings management to boost their earnings immediately prior to the IPO.[4] Sometimes, pre-IPO companies will even use financial manipulation or fraud to boost their performance and offer price, which reflects just how important IPOs can be for company executives, and indeed the severity of the information asymmetry problem.[5]

More evidence for the over-pricing of shares during an IPO comes in the form of management's concentrated selling of their company stocks as soon as the post-IPO lock-in period expires. Such executives are well aware that the shares are over-valued, so they aggressively unload them at the first opportunity. Of course, this usually marks the start of the shares' downward spiral.[6]

Despite ample evidence for the disappointing performance of IPO investments, many retail investors are still drawn to them. Because fortunes were made by investors with the foresight to buy shares in legendary companies such as Microsoft and Apple at the time of their IPOs, many investors delude themselves that they will enjoy similar success. Some of them also hope for IPO allotment, which means that they receive allotted pre-IPO shares immediately before the IPO. Profits are almost guaranteed for such lucky investors. However, it should be pointed out that retail investors have very little chance of receiving these pre-IPO shares, especially if there is a lot of interest in the IPO. They are more likely to receive them if the company has failed to generate much interest among the institutional investors, but in such instances the shares are scarcely worth buying, as they are highly likely to under-perform after the IPO.[7]

Unfortunately, all of these factors combine to leave retail investors with little chance of making money from IPOs.

China's IPO reform

Chinese investors are lured towards IPOs for another reason: they believe that other investors are desperate to buy IPO stocks.[8]

Because China currently enforces an approval-based IPO process, listing a company there is far more difficult than it is in most other capital markets. Every IPO is strictly regulated, and the supply of new offerings may even be constrained to shore up the A-shares market. As a result, interest in the relatively small number of IPOs is artificially stimulated. Given that entrepreneurs, private equity funds, and even local governments with stakes in pre-IPO companies all have incentives to sell their post-IPO shares after an attractive valuation, IPOs' initial over-pricing and subsequent under-performance are particularly striking in China. Earnings management, suppressing floating shares, window-dressing, and fraud are therefore common practices in the run-up to many Chinese IPOs.[9]

Consequently, many companies report disappointing earnings or even losses immediately after their IPOs, notwithstanding the rigorous scrutiny that such companies are obliged to undergo prior to the IPO. To make matters worse, regulatory loopholes allow corporate executives to escape punishment for their manipulation of IPO prices. Many senior executives know that their share allocations are heavily over-priced, so they resign from their corporate positions and liquidate their holdings in the company right after the IPO. Given that most Chinese IPO shares are priced at levels that are significantly higher than those of already-listed but otherwise comparable companies, retail investors in China's secondary market often buy over-priced stocks that are almost guaranteed to underperform in the long run.

The China Securities Regulatory Commission (CSRC) argues that the country's retail investors lack the ability and experience to distinguish between "good" and "bad" companies, so every proposed IPO must go through a supposedly stringent CSRC investigation. However, this has the unfortunate consequence that many Chinese retail investors believe that merely passing the approval process equates to receiving an endorsement from the CSRC. As a result, they do not exercise the necessary caution and due diligence when deciding whether the IPO is a sound investment. Such false confidence is so prevalent among Chinese retail investors that it could be argued that the CSRC investigations do more harm than good.

Furthermore, there is ample evidence that the CSRC itself lacks the ability to distinguish between "good" and "bad" companies, as investors have suffered considerable losses after investing in companies that have received clean bills of health during the approval process. For example, many Chinese investors bought shares in HuaRui FengDian, a manufacturer and installer of wind turbines, at more than 100 RMB per share on the day of the IPO. Shortly afterwards, the share price had fallen to just 10 RMB per share. Similarly, shares in PetroChina were priced at 40 RMB on the day of the company's IPO. They subsequently fell to 10 RMB per share and have failed to rise ever since.

Therefore, retail investors should not trust the judgment of the CSRC. They must do their own research into every seemingly attractive IPO and not succumb to over-confidence. Rather than falling for the common line that every IPO provides retail investors with a gilt-edged opportunity to claim a share in the wealth that a company with great potential will generate in the future, they must learn to see them for what they really are: wealth transfers from secondary market investors to entrepreneurs and early stage investors.[10]

Debt financing

Corporations that do not wish to launch an IPO may explore various debt financing options. One important aspect of this is that companies must decide whether to raise finance through long-term debt or short-term debt. In general, interest rates on the former tend to be higher than those on the latter, but they are guaranteed over a long period of time. This can be advantageous if interest rates rise over the lifetime of the loan, but a short-term loan would be the better option if interest rates subsequently fall. Hence, potential borrowers must estimate which way they think interest rates will move in the future and act accordingly.[11] Research has found that this is precisely what companies do: they dynamically evaluate various debt financing options and take investors' preferences and market conditions into account in order to maximize corporate value.

Variations in dividend payout

Corporate executives must make important decisions not only about financing, but also about payouts. Companies typically have the option of repaying their shareholders through dividends, share repurchases, or stock price appreciation. In theory, investors should gain the same amount from each of these alternatives, all else being equal, so they should be unconcerned about the form in which they receive their payout. However, companies with greater investment opportunities are likely to retain a large proportion of their earnings, whereas mature companies with ample cash flow are likely to pay out more of their earnings to investors.[12]

Unsurprisingly, many executives—in both nascent and mature companies—prefer to retain a large proportion of the company's earnings within the business, because this allows them to award themselves higher compensation packages and lucrative perquisites. However, there is a limit to how much they can do this without precipitating a shareholder revolt, so eventually they are obliged to pay out. Some companies regularly reward their shareholders through dividends. These not only provide investors with steady cash flow but also impose a degree of monitoring on corporate financial soundness. Therefore, most investors favor companies that pay regular dividends.[13]

Other companies have a tendency to start or stop paying dividends unexpectedly. Given that paying dividends or not has little impact on company cash flow or investors' returns, one might wonder why any business would choose to behave in this way. The answer is quite straightforward. In periods when shares in companies that pay dividends greatly out-perform those in companies that do not (such as the early 2000s, immediately after the internet bubble burst), ever more companies start to pay dividends in order to attract investors. In contrast, in periods when investors favor non-dividend-paying companies (such as during the internet bubble itself), ever more companies stop paying dividends. In other words, companies closely monitor and cater to investors' shifting preferences with respect to dividends.

In 2012 the CSRC recommended that companies should pay out minimum dividends, in the hope that such payments would improve corporate governance and enhance investor returns. However, this initiative largely fell on deaf ears, with few companies choosing to pay the recommended dividends. Consequently, the CSRC was forced to make the payment of cash dividends mandatory.

Companies have been similarly reluctant to engage in share repurchases. There is widespread suspicion that this is because Chinese corporate executives are well aware that their existing shares are over-valued, so they are unwilling to purchase any more at such inflated prices. Furthermore, Chinese investors, particularly retail investors, are more concerned with short-term stock price movements than long-term potential, so any company's efforts to improve its governance and long-term performance are unlikely to be rewarded by the market. Finally, because short selling and arbitrage are relatively rare in China, professional investors—such as hedge funds and mutual funds—are reluctant to help companies boost their value, which means they have less incentive to pay out dividends.

In summary, it seems that company executives cater to investors' preference for the highest possible corporate valuation, regardless of whether they are based in the East or the West.

Stock splits

At first glance, stock splits seem a rather puzzling phenomenon. Splitting a share in two and halving the share price would appear to be a pointless, cosmetic change that can have no bearing on a company's fundamentals. However, research has shown that investors are often enthralled when a company announces that it is planning to split its shares. Moreover, once the split has taken place, more retail investors are interested in buying the shares, resulting in a positive drift.[14]

Behavioral finance research suggests that investors prefer post-split stocks because they favor lower-priced shares, which they (falsely) interpret as trading at a bargain price.[15] There is also the simple point that stock split announcements tend to attract media attention, which leads some investors to contemplate investing in stocks that had not previously been on their radar.

Needless to say, executives at several listed companies have noticed investors' irrational reactions to stock splits and have initiated their own as a result. Of course, few companies split their shares in periods when high-priced stocks are out-performing low-priced stocks, but the number of splits increases dramatically when investors start to favor low-priced stocks.

Such share price adjustments are also a feature of IPOs. Pre-IPO companies have full control over how many shares to issue, which means they have considerable power over the price of each share at the time of the IPO. Researchers have found some predictable patterns in IPO pricing, with new shares priced in the relatively high price range when high-priced stocks are out-performing low-priced stocks, and vice versa. That is, executives clearly cater to investors' shifting preference for high or low stock prices in order to attract their attention in the run-up to an IPO.[16] For instance, during the 1998–2000 internet bubble, many companies offered relatively few shares at their IPOs in order to keep the price artificially high and attract feverish retail investor attention.

Name changes

In addition to mastering the best financing and payout strategies, corporate executives must learn how to use other tricks if they are to take full advantage of retail investors' often irrational investment decisions.

As we saw earlier, during the internet bubble, many companies added ".com" to their names in an attempt to convince investors that they were internet businesses.[17] Such name changes were rarely accompanied by fundamental changes to these companies' line of business or cash flow, the fundamentals that should dictate share price. And yet, on average, a company's share price would jump by about 70 percent after it added ".com" to its name. Clearly, then, this simple ploy attracted the attention—and capital—of many retail investors, especially inexperienced ones. Unfortunately, when the internet bubble burst, many of these companies lost more than 90 percent of their value, and some even filed for bankruptcy.[18]

As so often, though, investors' memories are short, and companies are always keen to exploit their gullibility. In 2015, a Chinese property developer and building materials supplier called Shanghai Duolun Industry changed its name to PiTuPi—a literal translation of "peer-to-peer"—at the height of the Chinese market's mania for "internet financing." The company's shares rose by 10 percent during its first day's trading under the new name, even though it has nothing to do with peer-to-peer lending, or indeed any other aspect of the financial services industry.[19]

Stocks with short, simple, easy-to-understand names also attract greater investor attention than those with complex names, and so enjoy better performance and higher valuations. Unsurprisingly, then, there are numerous examples of companies simplifying their names to take advantage of this particular example of investor bias.

Mutual fund name changes

As we saw earlier, it is not only listed companies that exploit investors' preference for certain names; mutual fund management companies do the same. The most common changes involve substituting "small cap" for "large cap" and vice versa, and substituting "value" for "growth" and vice versa. Of course, they tend to do this whenever investors start to display a preference for certain types of company. For example, during the internet bubble, when investors favored small-cap, high-growth stocks, many mutual funds included the words "small cap" and "growth" in their names. Once the bubble had burst, many of the same funds renamed themselves "large cap" and "value" in a bid to avoid any association with toxic internet stocks.

Such name changes are rarely accompanied by any change in a mutual fund's managers or even in its portfolio holdings. Put differently, they are totally cosmetic. However, they are also highly effective. Researchers have found that fund flow surges by an average of 50 percent in the six months after a fund changes its name.[20] This, then, is yet another example of canny executives monitoring investors' tastes closely, and then giving them precisely what they want.

Opening and closing mutual funds

In addition to changing their names, mutual fund companies will sometimes launch a new fund or close an existing one to cater to investor sentiment and demand.

Research shows that fund size tends to erode fund performance, so many mutual fund companies do not allow new clients to invest in their most famous, best-performing funds. Nevertheless, they will encourage the disappointed potential investor to put her money in one of their alternative funds, and she will often accept their kind offer. In other words, the prestigious fund serves as a powerful marketing tool for the company to boost the assets under its management.

Of course, closing funds to prospective clients means that fund management companies sacrifice some potentially lucrative management fees. Consequently, they may choose to reopen previously closed funds. These reopened funds frequently attract a great deal of attention as a result of investors' pent-up desire to gain access to them.[21] With no shortage of keen investors, the companies that offer them are also able to charge higher-than-average management fees.

Inevitably, though, once the excitement of gaining entry into a previously closed fund has worn off, many investors are left disappointed by poor returns, due in part to the fund's large size and the high management fees. On average, reopened funds rarely scale the heights they achieved when they were closed to new investors. Once again, then, we see that unscrupulous companies are able to profit from investors' irrational sentiment and enthusiasm by selling them poor products at exorbitant prices.

Notes

1 Derrien, F. 2005. IPO Pricing in "Hot" Market Conditions: Who Leaves Money on the Table? *Journal of Finance*, 60(1): 487–521.

2 Derrien, F. 2005. IPO Pricing in "Hot" Market Conditions: Who Leaves Money on the Table? *Journal of Finance*, 60(1): 487–521; Ljungqvist, A. and Wilhelm, W.J. 2003. IPO Pricing in the Dotcom Bubble. *Journal of Finance*, 58(2): 723–752.
3 Loughran, T. and Ritter, J.R. 1995. The New Issues Puzzle. *Journal of Finance*, 50(1): 23–51.
4 Wang, T.Y., Winton, A., and Yu, X. 2010. Corporate Fraud and Business Conditions: Evidence from IPOs. *Journal of Finance*, 65(6): 2255–2292.
5 Teoh, S.H., Welch, I., and Wong, T.J. 1998. Earnings Management and the Long-Run Market Performance of Initial Public Offerings. *Journal of Finance*, 53(6): 1935–1974.
6 Field, L.C. and Hanka, G. 2001. The Expiration of IPO Share Lockups. *Journal of Finance*, 56(2): 471–500; Ofek, E. and Richardson, M. 2003. Dotcom Mania: The Rise and Fall of Internet Stock Prices. *Journal of Finance*, 58(3): 1113–1138.
7 Megginson, W.L. and Weiss, K.A. 1991. Venture Capitalist Certification in Initial Public Offerings. *Journal of Finance*, 46(3): 879–903; Loughran, T. and Ritter, J. 2004. Why Has IPO Underpricing Changed over Time? Retrieved from https://site.warrington.ufl.edu/ritter/files/2015/06/Why-Has-IPO-Underpricing-Changed-Over-Time-2004.pdf.
8 Ritter, J.R. 1991. The Long-Run Performance of Initial Public Offerings. *Journal of Finance*, 46(1): 3–27.
9 Hong, H., Scheinkman, J., and Xiong, W. 2006. Asset Float and Speculative Bubbles. *Journal of Finance*, 61(3): 1073–1117.
10 http://stock.hexun.com/2011-08-17/132520755.html; http://finance.sina.com.cn/roll/20120116/022911207614.shtmls.
11 Baker, M. and Wurgler, J. 2002. Market Timing and Capital Structure. *Journal of Finance*, 57(1): 1–32; Wurgler, J. 2000. Financial Markets and the Allocation of Capital. *Journal of Financial Economics*, 58(1): 187–214.
12 Baker, M. and Wurgler, J. A. 2004. A Catering Theory of Dividends. *Journal of Finance*, 59(3): 1125–1165.
13 Baker, M. and Wurgler, J. 2004. Appearing and Disappearing Dividends: The Link to Catering Incentives. *Journal of Financial Economics*, 73(2): 271–288.
14 Ariely, D., Dhar, R., and Zhu, N. Why Individuals Favor Split Stocks. 2008. Working paper, Yale University.
15 Dhar, R., Goetzmann, W., Shepherd, S., and Zhu, N. 2007. The Impact of Clientele Change: Evidence from Stock Splits. Working paper.
16 Baker, M., Greenwood, R., and Wurgler. J. 2009. Catering through Nominal Share Prices. *Journal of Finance*, 64(6): 2559–2590.
17 Malkiel, B.J. 1999. A Random Walk down Wall Street: Including a Life-Cycle Guide to Personal Investing. New York: W.W. Norton & Company.
18 Cooper, M.J., Dimitrov, O., and Rau, P.R. 2001. A Rose.com by Any Other Name. *Journal of Finance*, 56(6): 2371–2388.
19 http://www.ejinsight.com/20150512-china-stock-names-misleading/.
20 Cooper, M.J., Gulen, H., and Rau, P.R. 2006. Changing Names with Style: Mutual Fund Name Changes and Their Effects on Fund Flows. *Journal of Finance*, 60(6): 2825–2858.
21 Bris, A., Gulen, H., Kadiyala, P., et al. 2007. Good Stewards, Cheap Talkers, or Family Men? The Impact of Mutual Fund Closures on Fund Managers, Flows, Fees, and Performance. *Review of Financial Studies*, 20(3): 953–982.

12
RISK MANAGMENT! RISK MANAGEMENT!

The origins of risk management

Cantor Fitzgerald (CF), established in 1945, is a specialist on Wall Street's fixed income market. By the late 1990s, its trading volume comprised between a fifth and a quarter of the total US bond market. The company's headquarters were located on Floors 101–105 of the North Tower of the World Trade Center, several floors above the point where terrorists crashed a plane into the building on September 11, 2011. The company lost approximately two-thirds of its employees that day, but over the next decade it gradually recovered and regained its position as one of the leading institutions in the US bond market.

What happened to CF, and how the company subsequently dealt with such an unexpected risk, has since become a popular case study among leading business schools around the world. Much of CF's own business relates to risk management, a discipline that began in the world of engineering, rather than finance. The original motivation was to manage potential risk in production processes and therefore allow enterprises to implement safer working environments, achieve steadier profit streams, and improve their preparation for extreme events.[1]

As the global geopolitical environment and the corporate business environment both become more complex, companies are facing greater challenges in risk management. When they occur, the scale of disasters is larger than ever, and the consequences more extreme. For example, on the night of December 2–3, 1984, more than 500,000 people were exposed to methyl isocyanate and other chemicals when they leaked from the Union Carbide pesticide plant in Bhopal, India. The final death toll was put at 3,787, and 558,125 people were injured. Twenty-six years later, the Fukushima tsunami in eastern Japan decimated a whole community and brought the country's nuclear industry to a halt.

Research into how to prepare for such disastrous events was undertaken exclusively by engineers in the early years of risk management. It was the 1970s before the field of finance started to borrow from these studies and attempted to apply their concepts and techniques to the management of investment risk. In the world of finance, "risk" is commonly defined as volatility in investment returns. If an investor were to invest money in a savings account for a guaranteed 3 percent interest every year, he would typically view his investment as "risk free." This is because he knows that he will make 3 percent each and every year, regardless of what happens to the economy. On the other hand, if he were to invest money in the stock market, he might make a profit of 10 percent or he might lose 5 percent over the course of the year. Clearly, then, this is a more risky type of investment because the investor has no way of knowing whether he will gain or lose money.

Finance theory assumes that investors prefer high returns and low risk. Therefore, it assumes a positive relationship between return and risk: high-risk securities should have the potential to generate higher returns for investors. Otherwise, why would anyone choose to hold high-risk assets? However, typically, investors focus far more on the returns rather than the risk when deciding whether to buy a particular stock. If you were to ask an investor what he made from his investments last year, he would probably provide a quite accurate estimate. On the other hand, if you were to ask how risky those investments were, he would probably roll his eyes and admit he had no idea.

Two factors contribute to this lack of understanding of—and interest in—risk. First, as we have discussed throughout this book, investors tend to focus on the positive rather than the negative when contemplating the future. Given that risk fits squarely in the negative column, most investors either consciously or subconsciously choose to ignore it. Second, risks are defined in quadratic terms in math, whereas returns are defined in linear terms. This makes it far more difficult for investors—at least those who are not mathematicians—to develop an intuitive understanding of the true nature of risk. Hence, some of them abandon any attempt to do so and instead focus solely on returns.

This is why the Sharpe ratio—a ratio of return to risk—is so important, because it can capture the relative risk-adjusted returns of various investment opportunities.

The price of risk: the Sharpe ratio

The Sharpe ratio was named after William Sharpe, a Nobel laureate who formulated the idea of dividing the excess returns of an investment (the extra profit that is earned by investing in a risky rather than a risk-free product) by the volatility of the same investment. His aim was to "standardize" the risk when evaluating the performance of rival stocks or fund managers. The idea is that the Sharpe ratio allows investors to control for differences in the riskiness of alternative investments or strategies; therefore, they should be able to evaluate the relative attractiveness of each alternative.

Some hedge funds boast Sharpe ratios of over 200 percent, meaning that for every unit of volatility of the investment strategy, the hedge fund generates two units of returns. That is a pretty good risk–return trade-off (although, of course, investors' net returns will be considerably lower once management and incentive fees are taken into account).[2] As to long-only investment opportunities, many international mutual funds generate Sharpe ratios of 0.4–0.5, meaning that they generate 0.4–0.5 returns for every unit of risk (i.e. average annualized returns of 12 percent, minus a risk-free rate of return of 4 percent, divided by annualized volatility of about 18 percent in the US equities market).

The Chinese equities market is less attractive. The average annualized returns in the Chinese market are higher, at about 15 percent, but the annualized volatility is more than 40 percent, which generates a Sharpe ratio of about 0.2 (the annualized risk-free rate of return is about 5 percent)—much lower than those of many international markets. Clearly, then, the problem with the Chinese market is not low returns but high volatility.

According to the "rule of 72," annualized returns of 12 percent can allow an investor to double her original investment in six years. However, if those annualized returns are accompanied by high risk, not only may the investor be unable to double her original investment; she also runs the risk of losing much of her money. Say the investor loses 50 percent of her principal in the first year, it will be a long time before she even breaks even, let alone doubles her money. Such an example may be extreme, but it certainly illustrates the importance of volatility—and hence risk—in long-term investment. Therefore, most retail investors should understand that reducing their exposure to risk can be just as important as increasing their returns.

Risk and uncertainty

Now that we are familiar with the concept of risk, it is time to introduce another rather confusing concept: uncertainty. One might ask if there are any differences between the two, given that all risks are uncertain. However, the notion of uncertainty implies a greater lack of knowledge. In risk management, the term "risk" is often used when referring to something with a known statistical distribution but no firm idea of precisely what will happen within that distribution. In contrast, "uncertainty" implies that the distribution itself is a mystery. Some commentators argue that the 2008 global financial crisis was caused in part by large financial institutions confusing the two concepts and becoming over-confident in their risk management models as a result, which meant that they failed to foresee the "once in a century" crisis.[3]

In his influential book *Black Swan*, Nissim Taleb explains the differences between risk and uncertainty and offers suggestions for how each should be managed.[4] He believes that risk management should be developed into a risk-respecting culture which accepts that every risk management model has its limitations because of the inherent uncertainty of the world's financial markets. Precisely because of this uncertainty, households and corporations should leave themselves with "safety margins" when investing or speculating, and both should understand the limitations of statistics and predictive models. According to Taleb, the risks that can be measured and estimated with existing models are relatively easy to manage. However, we should be much more concerned about the far greater risks that we are unable to predict. These can be far more devastating, as the global financial crisis and the Fukushima tsunami have proved in recent years. Furthermore, sometimes the "long tail" or "fat tail" nature of risks make them much more difficult to manage than was previously thought.

Finally, increasingly sophisticated risk management tools may add to the problem by generating a false sense of confidence and security, which in turn can encourage greater risk-taking than might otherwise be the case. That is, ironically, advances in risk management techniques can make people increasingly blasé about risk.

Risk induced by success

The 2008 global financial crisis revealed that risk may not be quite as random as some simplistic quantitative models might suggest. In fact, it proved that the activities of private investors, financial institutions, corporations, and governments can have a dramatic impact on the level of risk in a market.

Say a gambler takes 100 dollars into the casino one morning, gets lucky, and wins a further 900 dollars by noon. If his wallet had contained 1,000 dollars that morning, the gambler surely would not have decided to bet all of it during his visit to the casino. However, given that he feels the 900 dollars he has won is "house money," he decides to take greater risks—in the hope of higher returns—after lunch. In such circumstances, the chances are that the gambler will lose all 1,000 dollars in the afternoon, leaving himself 100 dollars down on the day. This extreme example shows that people's risk-taking behavior can be easily affected by personal experience.

Of course, risk profiles can change for other reasons too. Look at what the financial institutions did prior to the global financial crisis. Many of them purchased credit default swap (CDS) contracts to hedge their potential losses from toxic real estate investments, which led to even greater speculation because the traders felt they could not lose: if their speculative gambles paid off, they would earn millions of dollars in bonuses; if they failed, a third party (typically an insurance company or a rival hedge fund) would pick up the tab. Hence, by taking full—if not excessive—advantage of financial innovations that were originally designed to improve risk management in the financial sector, numerous financial institutions dramatically increased the whole sector's exposure to risk and therefore the likelihood that an unprecedented crisis would develop.[5]

Risk due to financial innovation

While the twentieth century was known as the century of technological innovation, some people have suggested that the twenty-first will be the century of financial innovation. Indeed, innovations in the financial sector have already enabled more people than ever before to afford houses, cars, college educations, and so on.

However, the other side of the same coin is that we are also suffering more frequent, and deeper, financial crises than ever before. The 1987 stock market crash, the US savings and loans crisis of the early 1990s, the Southeast Asian financial crisis of 1997, the internet bubble of 1999–2000, the global financial crisis of 2008, and the European sovereign debt crisis of 2010 all point to the fact that we are living in the most volatile financial market in human history. And financial innovations must shoulder some of the blame. Bill Gross—also known as the "Bond King"—believes that this pattern is here to stay, terming this low-return, high-volatility market paradigm the "new norm."

Perhaps surprisingly, even though financial innovations have helped to diversify risk among more investors and more markets over longer periods of time, they have done nothing to eliminate risk itself. Instead, such innovations have resulted in increasing opaqueness in information disclosure and a false sense of security among investors, both of which have prompted more risky behavior.

As we saw earlier in the book, Long Term Capital Management (LTCM), the legendary hedge fund that was founded by two of Wall Street's top traders, ex-Federal Reserve senior officials, and several leading scientists and researchers, used quantitative models to generate some impressive returns during its first five years of operation. Its arbitrage model once calculated that the chance of the fund losing more than 5 percent over the course of a single trading day was less than 1 in 20 million. However, as the fund managers' confidence in their models increased, they started to take ever greater risks. Then came the default in Russian sovereign debt in the fall of 1998, which generated a massive surge in flight-to-safety trades—the exact opposite of what LTCM's model had predicted. The exodus of arbitrage traders and fall in market liquidity caused LTCM to lose over 90 percent of its asset value in a matter of weeks. The collapse was so massive that the US Federal Reserve had to team up with almost every leading US financial institution to bail out LTCM.

Such incidents reveal that, no matter how sophisticated the mathematics or models may be, it is the people who use them, and how they choose to interpret them, who have the greatest role to play in generating high returns or spectacular failures.

The growth of the credit card industry provides more evidence of the potential dangers of financial innovation. The emergence of credit cards has undoubtedly stimulated growth in consumer finance and facilitated more consumer spending and enjoyment. However, many households have fallen victim to their high interest rates and have ended up in personal bankruptcy. Furthermore, some unscrupulous banks and other lending institutions deliberately encourage households that lack financial literacy to build up their debt, which induces irresponsible consumption decisions and destroys such households' credit records.

Finally, as we have seen in previous chapters, online trading has made it much easier and quicker for retail investors to trade on the stock market. However, most of these investors lack the skill to exploit the advantages that online trading can confer, and indeed make frequent and speculative trades that lose them money over the long term.

In summary, financial innovations and technological development have not only done little to improve the management of risk; they have also created new risks of their own.

Risk due to individual behavioral bias

One key difference between financial risk management and risk management in engineering is the degree to which people must be taken into consideration. Risk management in engineering typically considers machinery, factories, pipelines, and the natural environment, whereas financial risk management is much more concerned with human beings, and especially their sometimes irrational behavior and biases. Unsurprisingly, merely identifying risks in dynamic financial markets is much more difficult than identifying risks in a static factory, and that is before the "animal spirit" that may move a whole market is taken into consideration. Moreover, risk assessors face even greater challenges when they attempt to measure the risks they have identified on account of the behavioral biases that we have discussed throughout this book—over-confidence, self-attribution, the illusion of control, framework thinking, representativeness bias, loss aversion, and mood.

Greed and fear are widely regarded as two major enemies of astute financial decision making. To some extent, greed is a reflection of the over-confidence that has been discussed throughout this book. People are often too confident in their own predictive ability, so they feel little need to exercise disciplined risk management. Similarly, investors' aversion to loss after suffering an early setback can distort their subsequent investment decisions, which in turn can lead to more irrational behavior and poor choices.

Representativeness bias causes investors to project short-term experiences into long-term trends, which serves to exacerbate financial market volatility and generate persistent and additional risks. In addition, framework thinking causes investors to focus on individual stocks rather than the whole portfolio, let alone the whole market. Such framework-dependent thinking can shift quickly, which leads investors to make temporally inconsistent decisions.

Risk due to corporate culture

China Aviation Oil

China Aviation Oil (CAO) specialized in trading aviation oil options. The company made a profit in 2013, but then suffered a modest loss of 5.8 million dollars the following year. However, rather than managing the risk and absorbing the loss, the CEO, Chen Jiulin, continued to gamble that the price of aviation oil would fall. Instead, the oil price continued to escalate and CAO's losses followed suit, eventually peaking at over 500 million dollars. The company filed for bankruptcy and Chen Jiulin was sentenced to four years and three months in prison for securities fraud.

Ironically, CAO's involvement in aviation oil trading was originally motivated by a desire to hedge against risk. However, the management team convinced themselves that they had identified a pattern in aviation oil price fluctuation, then made the fatal decision to speculate heavily on the basis of their "discovery." At first, in 2013, everything went according to plan: the market corresponded to the pattern, CAO made a substantial profit from its trades, and the management team collected generous bonuses. They also became more confident than ever that they could beat the market. But then the market started to diverge from the pattern, and the profits turned to losses. Rather than believe the evidence that was before their eyes, however, the management team kept faith in their model right until the point when they ran the company into the ground. This is a classic example of how the absence of diligent risk management within an organization's corporate culture can lead to the collapse of the whole enterprise.

Several years earlier, CITIC Pacific—a subsidiary of the Chinese state-owned enterprise (SOE) CITIC and a listed company in Hong Kong—had gone through something very similar, only on a much larger scale. Motivated initially by a desire to hedge its investments in Australia, CITIC Pacific started trading Australian dollars on the world's currency markets. At first, the company profited from these trades and confidence in the wisdom of its position—that the Australian dollar's seemingly inexorable rise would continue—started to grow. This persuaded CITIC Pacific to sign ever more contracts with major financial institutions around the world in which it invariably bet on a strengthening Australian dollar. However, a few months later, at the peak of the global financial crisis in the fall of 2008, the Australian dollar started to fall like a stone and CITIC Pacific suffered 15.5 billion Hong Kong dollars' worth of losses. Consequently, the company's share price fell from 30 to less than 5 Hong Kong dollars. To add insult to injury, CITIC Pacific's bullish speculation on the Australian dollar soon proved to be entirely justified when the currency reached unprecedented heights less than a year later. However, because the company had invested in particularly complex derivatives known as "accumulators," it had to pull out of the market before its gamble started to generate profits or even break even. It was CITIC Pacific's initial currency trading success which persuaded the management team to invest in accumulators, which do not require upfront payment but do involve considerable risk.

Both CAO and CITIC Pacific seemed to forget what prompted them to start trading in the first place before they headed down the path of no return. If a company fully recognizes and understands risk, it should always be willing and able to hedge against such risk, regardless of the outcome of its hedging trades. However, both of these enterprises let short-term profits dictate their subsequent risk exposure and trading activities, so they both fundamentally misunderstood the purpose of risk management.

Second, CAO and CITIC Pacific, as well as many other Chinese companies that have suffered significant losses since 2008, such as Shanghai Airlines and the China Railway Construction Company (CRCC), have fallen victim to representativeness bias. Initial successes led all of these companies to believe that they had found a foolproof way to predict market fluctuations. Hence, they all speculated without first implementing proper stop-loss or risk-control mechanisms. As a result, the losses they incurred when the market turned unexpectedly were far greater than they might have been.

Finally, both CAO and CITIC Pacific had very weak corporate governance and minimal checks and balances between their business units and risk management units. All major decisions were taken by a single person, and no dissenting opinions or propositions that may have limited the losses were entertained during the decision making process. In this regard, both companies are once again typical of many other Chinese SOEs whose risk management cultures, techniques, and practice are in urgent need of upgrading.

Notes

1. http://dealbook.nytimes.com/2011/09/03/the-survivor-who-saw-the-future-for-cantor-fitzgerald/.
2. http://en.wikipedia.org/wiki/Sharpe_ratio.
3. http://en.wikipedia.org/wiki/Knightian_uncertainty.
4. Taleb, N. 2010. *The Black Swan*. New York: Random House.
5. Keys, B.J., Seru, A., and Vig, V. 2012. Lender Screening and the Role of Securitization: Evidence from Prime and Subprime Mortgage Markets. *Review of Financial Studies*, 25(7): 2071–2108.

13

REGULATION AND GOVERNMENT DECISION MAKING

The behavioral biases of governments and regulators

It is important to point out that many of the behavioral biases that we have discussed in this book are not limited to individuals; organizations are affected by them, too. That should come as no surprise, because organizations are made up of individuals, and their decisions are made by individuals. However, the decision making process within an organization is more complex for two reasons. First, there is the agency problem—when principals and agents hold different objectives and agendas. Instead of thinking solely about what is in the best interests of the organization, the people in charge of the decision making process may want to maximize their personal benefits and satisfaction, too. Much of the literature on corporate governance deals with this topic. Of course, as an organization increases in size, the costs of information collection, communication, and coordination all increase exponentially, which exacerbates the difficulty of making well-informed and correct decisions.[1]

Second, and possibly more importantly, decision makers' behavior tends to shift in the context of collective decision making. For example, the famous Stanford prison experiment of the early 1970s confirmed that people make far more extreme decisions when they are placed in a collective decision making situation than when they are able to act as individuals.[2] Experiments at Yale University around the same time similarly showed that people within the context of an authoritarian hierarchy tend to make extreme or even cruel decisions when compared to individuals who are free to act as they please.[3]

Follow-up research revealed that individuals gravitate towards the collective opinion or decisions that an existing member of the decision making team has already reached. They also tend to focus on previously discussed issues and neglect those that have not been debated. In addition, because a great deal of time is devoted to information collection and communication in collective decision making processes, there is usually little time to discuss the relative merits of each alternative.[4]

At the same time, because most people wish to avoid personal confrontation, collective decision making is likely to generate consensus. Also, because almost every individual in a group decision making context feels that he or she is only partly responsible for the decision, the members of the group tend to become less committed and put less effort into identifying the best option.

In summary, despite a group's best intentions, collective decision making often proves to be far more challenging and counterproductive than originally envisaged. Consequently, the decisions that are reached by commercial organizations and government agencies may be unnecessarily extreme and/or incorrect.

Over-confidence: easy monetary policy

Military leaders are notoriously over-confident about the strength of their defenses. For instance, in ancient China, generations of leaders put their faith in the Great Wall, only to see it fail to halt numerous invasions from the north. Similarly, in the 1930s France spent a fortune on the Maginot Line in preparation for a German invasion, and the country's military hierarchy expressed supreme confidence that it would prove impassable. However, German troops circumvented the whole system by the simple expedient of attacking through the Ardennes Forest and reached Paris in a matter of weeks. A few decades later, Israel built up its defenses to guard against Egyptian attack. When the offensive began, the Egyptian army used high-pressure water cannons to blast through the much-vaunted Bar Lev defense line in a few hours.

But it is not only generals who are susceptible to over-confidence. Central bankers and financial market regulators have proved similarly complacent. As the former chairman of the US Federal Reserve Paul Volcker once put it, "The easiest thing for central banks is easy money."[5] As long as inflation stays within the official target zone, many central bankers admit that supporting economic growth remains their primary objective. And they have attempted to promote this through easy money policy. For example, another former chairman of the Federal Reserve, Alan Greenspan, was known to favor the stimulation of economic growth and stock market performance through active monetary policy. He engineered one of the largest—and once thought to be the greatest—balancing acts in economic history by employing this policy to boost both the US and the global economy, as well as stock markets around the world. During his tenure, he also used subtle adjustments of US monetary policy to avert economic slowdowns in the wake of the Southeast Asian financial crisis of 1997 and the dotcom crash a few years later. This led many commentators to laud Greenspan as a maestro of monetary policy and possibly the greatest central banker of all time.[6] Some even suggested that his easy money policy solved the riddle of how to boost economic growth and employment without suffering inevitable inflation and the development of asset bubbles. The adulation continued until the summer of 2007.

What happened thereafter, however, served as a loud wake-up call to everyone who argued that Greenspan's financial innovation fundamentally changed the risk-to-return trade-off in monetary policy. It transpired that the easy money policy of the early 2000s not only provided strong incentives to speculate on real estate and related securities, but also altered market participants' perceptions of risk and expected returns. As the housing markets in the United States and many other developed economies reached their peak (and homes were less affordable than they had ever been), it became clear that the easy money policy had generated one of the largest bubbles in economic history. A government's very good intentions to shore up the economy and the financial markets ultimately induced unexpected and undesirable shifts in the market's mentality and boldness, which in turn almost destroyed the global financial system. As Jean de La Fontaine once said, "One often meets one's destiny on the path one takes to avoid it."[7]

Representativeness bias: the ban on short selling

During the ensuing global financial crisis, stock market regulators in the United States and many other countries quickly changed tack and adopted another policy in order to avert total market meltdown and the collapse of financial institutions' share prices—they imposed a ban on short selling.

Short selling—selling securities that one does not actually own and then buying them later (hopefully) at a lower price—dates all the way back to the Dutch stock market of the seventeenth century. Over the centuries, regulators and the rest of the market have tended to discriminate against investors who engage in this practice, to such an extent that short sellers in Napoleon's France faced the prospect of a year in prison. Even today, especially during periods of financial crisis, they are viewed as troublemakers rather than skillful, insightful market players. For instance, George Soros was widely criticized for making a fortune through short selling during the collapse of sterling in the early 1990s and the 1997 Southeast Asian financial crisis, as were Jim Chanos for profiting from the 1999–2001 internet bubble and John Paulson for short selling at the height of the 2007–2008 global financial crisis. In contrast, investors who make their fortunes through more traditional buy-and-hold investment strategies, such as Warren Buffett and Peter Lynch, are praised as financial geniuses.

Governments and regulators are understandably concerned that short sellers benefit from the dissemination of negative news that causes the market to drop substantially. And, granted, some short-term short sellers have used this tactic to drive down share prices to such an extent that individual companies and even the market as a whole have suffered. However, there are just as many examples of them playing the role of whistleblower and alerting the market to over-valuation and even financial fraud, as they did during the 1997 Southeast Asian financial crisis, the 1999–2001 internet bubble, and the 2007–2008 global financial crisis.

In a study spanning more than a decade and encompassing more than 40 countries, my colleagues and I conducted systematic analyses of short selling practices and their impact on the world's financial markets. We found no convincing evidence that banning the practice stabilizes stock markets or makes them less likely to fall. Indeed, we learned that such bans have the opposite effect, because they reduce investors' incentives to reveal information to the market and hence cause it to operate in a less efficient way.

Yet again, then, regulators' good intentions prove misguided when they come up against rational market forces. A ban on short selling has the effect of reducing the circulation of negative information and opinions in the financial markets. Hence, it serves as a form of implicit governmental support for those markets. However, this kind of governmental interference in the markets can have unintended consequences by prompting market participants to behave in unexpected ways, which usually generates greater risk and instability in the long run. For example, Alessandro Beber (Cass Business School) and Marco Pagano (Center for Studies in Economics and Finance) found little evidence that the ban on short selling was effective in stabilizing stock prices during the 2008 global financial crisis.[8] Instead, their study found clear evidence of declining liquidity and price discovery in the stock market, which damaged investors' confidence.

The illusion of control: barriers to entering the Chinese equities market and the Chinese housing market

Governments often exhibit a form of over-confidence by over-estimating their control over the economy and industrial policy. This led to an ongoing debate over the effectiveness of economic planning throughout the twentieth century. There was considerable support for central planning in the second half of the century, especially during the 1970s, when the Western economies experienced a period of prolonged stagnation while the Soviet Union seemed to be thriving. This, along with Japan's postwar "economic miracle," convinced many commentators that governments have the power to achieve outstanding economic growth through careful planning.

However, when the economies of the Soviet Union and its satellite states collapsed, and the Japanese economy entered two decades of stagnation, the limitations of central planning started to become apparent. It seemed that attempts to smooth economic cycles and extend periods of economic growth invariably ended up in punishing crises and extended recessions. In fact, the harder the policy makers tried to help the economy, the greater distortion and damage they would inflict on it.

IPOs in China

As we saw earlier, all initial public offerings (IPOs) in China must be approved by the regulatory authority (the China Securities Regulatory Commission (CSRC)) before they are allowed to proceed. Different from registration-based IPO processes in other countries, China's IPO process entails substantive investigations into the suitability and sustainability of the company in question, a task that is usually left to the market elsewhere.

Furthermore, the CSRC often uses the IPO process as a means to moderate market sentiment and the relationship between supply and demand for listed companies. So, when the CSRC decides that the market is rising too fast, it typically accelerates its investigations in order to increase the supply of securities and dampen speculation. By contrast, when it decides that the market needs a boost, it slows down—or even temporarily halts—all of its IPO investigations to limit the supply of securities in the belief that this will stabilize market sentiment. The CSRC claims that it adopted this approach because it protects retail investors who lack the experience to discern good from bad companies. However, most commentators believe that its principal purpose is to regulate the market.

To make matters worse, many Chinese retail investors who know little about the fundamentals of IPO companies are persuaded to invest heavily in them because they believe that any company which has passed the supposedly rigorous CSRC investigation must be good. Unfortunately, this means that they tend to buy vastly over-priced IPO shares and then suffer considerable losses, many of which are never recovered.

China's housing market

Some commentators believe that China's housing market is the largest bubble in economic history.[9] Certainly, given the price-to-rent ratio, the price-to-income ratio, and even absolute prices, it is currently one of the most expensive markets in the world. In a bid to constrain the rising house prices, the Chinese government has adopted a number of "curb policies" which limit real estate purchases in certain cities to those people who meet a set of stringent requirements (often linked to the applicant's hukou and social security status). However, whenever these curb policies are relaxed or removed, house prices immediately surge upwards dramatically due to pent-up demand. As a result, ever more people are now complaining that the curb policies themselves have artificially distorted the relationship between supply and demand in China's housing market and hold them responsible for the widespread assumption that prices will continue to rise forever.

In some extreme cases, Chinese buyers have filed for divorce in order to circumvent a particular curb policy. This became so prevalent in 2015 and 2016 that government agencies started issuing quotas on the number of divorces that they would grant.

Bubbles generated by government policy

At this point, it may be useful to examine China's economic policy and growth "miracle" from the behavioral finance perspective.

Over the past few decades, China's economy has arguably been the fastest growing yet least understood in the world. By utilizing a large army of cheap labor, unleashing labor productivity and entrepreneurship, and increasing capital input, the country has achieved extraordinary domestic growth that has drastically improved standards of living while also increasing China's economic, political, and military influence around the globe. However, restructuring of the world's economic and financial systems in the wake of the 2008 global financial crisis, rising labor costs, falling investment returns, deteriorating environmental conditions, and diminishing natural resources mean that China's economy is now facing unprecedentedly complicated challenges.

Governmental guarantees have undoubtedly provided tremendous and highly valuable impetus to China's economic growth over the past three decades, but they could also be held responsible for the challenges that the country currently faces. By reviewing the potential risks that are involved in various types of governmental guarantee, it may be possible to identify solutions that will help China achieve sustainable, high-quality economic growth over the long term.

As small- and medium-sized businesses have found it increasingly difficult to access financing amid slowing economic growth and declines in corporate earnings, China's government, corporations, and households have all witnessed considerable increases in their respective leverage ratios in recent years. The country's debt problem has attracted ever more attention from other governments, scholars, corporations, and investors around the world. In the short term, debt financing has the clear advantages of lower financing costs and easier financing procedures, as well as the potential to catapult the growth of enterprises and even countries. However, the potential for default or bankruptcy, and the substantial costs and reputational damage both entail, should limit the debt capacity of any enterprise or country.

To some extent, Japan's "lost decades" and the bursting of its housing and stock market bubbles were due to over-leveraging among Japanese corporations and households during the boom years of the 1970s and 1980s. As in Japan in the 1990s, banks now dominate the Chinese financial sector. Even though the Chinese bond market remains relatively under-developed in comparison to that of Japan or even China's own stock market, there has been significant growth in "bond-like" Chinese investment products in recent years. Trust products, wealth management products (WMPs), and many of the products that are sold by so-called "internet finance" platforms all closely resemble fixed income products that are available in other financial markets. Unlike the fixed income products that are offered in the West, however, many of China's bond-like products carry implicit guarantees from their underwriters, the regulators, and, ultimately, the Chinese government. Many investors believe that the financial institutions are keen to protect their reputations, the regulators are keen to advance their careers, and the Chinese government is keen to maintain social stability, so it is in the interests of all three to ensure that investors are not exposed to any sort of risk when investing in such products. Hence, the investors feel free to focus all their attention on finding the product that will generate the highest returns. Unfortunately, this "heads I win, tails you lose" mentality has resulted in aggressive speculation in the Chinese housing market, stock market, shadow banking markets, and nascent internet finance field.

Consequently, asset prices are in serious danger of rising far above their fundamental values and forming a bubble.

Even more worryingly, local government financing vehicles (LGFV) have relied heavily upon land sales and real estate development in the form of trust products and WMPs with implicit guarantees. Moreover, many products that were originally considered high risk and had unpromising returns have become "safe," attractive investments due to financial restructuring and the development of shadow banking products. Whenever Chinese investors see the implicit guarantees that underpin these products, they come to believe that the government will shoulder all of the risk and therefore invest heavily in them. However, should the government decide to withdraw its guarantees—for instance, if it decides that it is exposing itself to too much risk—the shadow banking sector, investors' high returns, and the cheap financing that many state-owned enterprises (SOEs) and LGFVs have enjoyed over recent years will all be seriously impacted, casting dark clouds over China's future economic growth.

Furthermore, the myriad challenges that China's economy is currently facing— such as the slowing of economic growth, serious over-capacity in many sectors, escalating debt among SOEs and in local government, and excessive volatility in many investment fields—may all be explained by Chinese investors' willingness to speculate and take excessive risks over the past few years. Indeed, to some extent, these challenges are direct consequences of the bursting of a number of bubbles that were encouraged by implicit guarantees.

Everyone acknowledges that the Chinese government's policies have helped stimulate high-speed economic growth since the 1990s, but they have also had the less desirable outcomes of shifting the risk preferences of investors and enterprises and transforming the social allocation of risk and capital, the trade-off between risk and return, and the balance between short-term and long-term objectives. Many of the Chinese financial sector's current dilemmas—such as small- and medium-sized enterprises' (SMEs') inability to secure financing, the migration of capital away from industry and into investment and speculation, and the growth of numerous mini-bubbles—are aspects of the "guaranteed bubble" phenomenon that has become increasingly prevalent throughout China.

On the one hand, it is understandable that China's leaders remain committed to stimulate rapid economic growth because of the benefits it will bring in terms of improved living standards and enhanced international status. On the other hand, if the government is truly committed to the dictum "Let the market play the decisive role in resource allocation"—as enunciated at the Third Plenum—investors must learn to shoulder more of the risks of their own investment decisions, and the government must gradually withdraw the implicit guarantees it has provided for various enterprises and investment products.

Only when investors are allowed—indeed required—to take full responsibility for the inherent risks of their personal investments, without the safety net of various implicit and explicit guarantees from the government, will they start to set realistic goals for the rate of economic growth and investment returns. And only when that happens will the market start to play its proper, dominant role in screening and monitoring, and in the efficient allocation of resources and capital. By contrast, if the guarantee bubble phenomenon is allowed to continue, investment speculation and the misallocation of resources and capital will only increase.

As the border between the state and the market, the trade-off between risk and return, and the balance between the present and the future become more transparent and clearly defined, we will start to resolve the problems of over-capacity, worsening debt, deteriorating SOE performance, SMEs' financing difficulties, and the consequent systemic financial risks that seem so pervasive at present.

Failure is the solution (to the Chinese shadow banking problem)

In January 2014, it became apparent that one of the China Credit Trust Company's trust products was running the risk of default. The product was backed by assets in the once-successful Shanxi Zhenfu Energy Group, a coal company that had borrowed 3 billion yuan (about 500 million US dollars) from the China Credit Trust Company and the ICBC bank, but Zhenfu was now in financial difficulties. It had borrowed the money to expand its production capacity in the hope that coal prices would rise. However, as the US Federal Reserve started to wind down its program of quantitative easing, coal prices started to fall, and Zhenfu was forced to shut down production.

Of course, many similar companies around the world have defaulted on their loans in recent years, but the Zhenfu story is unusual because the China Credit Trust Company insisted that it acted solely as a distribution channel for the trust product that was linked to the mining company. It claimed that the true holder and guarantor of the product was the Shanxi branch of ICBC, China's largest bank and one of the largest in the world, in terms of assets and revenue. Meanwhile, ICBC insisted that the product was entirely the responsibility of the China Credit Trust Company, so ICBC was under no obligation to pick up the tab if Zhenfu was unable to repay the principal or the interest on its loan.

This episode attracted widespread attention partly because the symbiotic system between China's banks and trust companies—also known as the formal and shadow banking sectors, respectively—had worked very well up to this point, so nobody had bothered to work out what to do if the collaborative relationship suddenly collapsed, as happened between the China Credit Trust Company and ICBC.

The incident set a very interesting precedent for China's entire shadow banking sector. The sector, which offers many high-yield trust products and WMPs, has mushroomed over recent years. (For instance, the China Credit Trust Company and ICBC promised their wealthy clients returns of 9.5–11.5 percent per year if they invested in products that were linked to the Zhenfu coal mine.) Indeed, by 2014, it was responsible for a large proportion of the financing for small- and medium-sized Chinese enterprises, as well as investments in many industries with severe over-capacity, many local government debts, and local government financing vehicles. Such products have become tremendously popular not only because they offer very attractive returns (sometimes as high as 18 percent per year), but also because many investors believe that they are extremely safe. Although every product's prospectus stipulates that the security of the principal is not guaranteed, the trust companies and their commercial bank partners *do* guarantee the safety of such investments because of regulatory and reputational concerns.

Moreover, these implicit guarantees are strengthened if the products are used to finance local government debts or financing vehicles. Although there is no evidence of any local government ever promising to assume full responsibility for the risk of investing in such a product, most investors still believe that they would do so in the event of a default. In fact, given that many local governments are now indebted up to the hilt and running into financial difficulties, investors have started to set their sights on central government in the (possibly mistaken) belief that it will bail out any local government that runs the risk of defaulting on its loans.

Such assumptions lie at the heart of the country's escalating shadow banking problem. The Chinese Banking Regulatory Committee (CBRC) has recently discussed the need to tackle this problem or at least make it more transparent. With disclosure of the related financials and fiduciary responsibilities increasingly shouldered by various involved parties, investors are now able to access more information on the viability and sustainability of the shadow banking sector's many trust products and WMPs. Probably more importantly, though, the regulators are also gaining a clearer picture of just how serious the shadow banking and local government debt problem has become in China. According to a recent round of auditing conducted by the China Audit Authority, local governments' liabilities rose by 70 percent over the course of just three years to stand at the alarming level of 20 trillion RMB. Although that figure was largely in line with expectations, the pace at which the debt had increased and the diminishing sources of fiscal revenue have led many commentators to express concerns about the soundness of Chinese local governments' financial situations.

As we have seen, the shadow banking sector has financed much of this debt via trust products and WMPs. Some of these products are fundamentally unsound, but the trust companies are able to market them as "safe" because of their implicit guarantees. In reality, they bear many similarities to the collateralized debt obligations (CDOs) that played such a significant role in precipitating the 2008 global financial crisis.

To make matters even worse, implicit guarantees have permeated many other parts of the Chinese economy. For instance, over-capacity and the resulting pressure it exerts on producers' prices—a problem that has started to haunt the Chinese economy in recent years—is largely due to reckless investment in industries such as cement, steel and iron, and solar energy. Investors were able to pour money into these sectors via products such as the one distributed by the China Credit Trust Company and ICBC, and they were eager to do so because of the widespread belief that local governments would provide bailouts if everything turned sour. Such assumptions were surely strengthened when Shanxi province allowed the ailing

Zhenfu coal mine to restart production, and when Jiangxi province bailed out the solar panel producer Jiangxi Saiwei. Likewise, investors in the Chinese real estate and A-shares markets firmly believe that the government will never allow prices to fall in either market, for fear of the protests and civil unrest that would ensue. However strong such beliefs may be, investors must learn that the economy follows its own rules, and prolonged distortion of prices or productivity runs the risk of generating bubbles and steering the country towards recession.

The only way in which investors will learn this truth is if some failing products are allowed to default. Only by sustaining losses will investors come to understand the true nature of risk and adjust their expectations accordingly. Only when their expectations become more realistic will the market system set a proper price on risk. And only then will central and local government and enterprises start to invest and secure financing in a reasonable and responsible manner.

Maybe Steve Jobs was right when he said, "Death is very likely the single best invention of life." Similarly, failure may be the only solution to China's shadow banking problem.

Notes

1. http://en.wikipedia.org/wiki/Group_decision_making.
2. https://en.wikipedia.org/wiki/Stanford_prison_experiment.
3. Moscovici, S. and Zavalloni, M. 1969. The Group as a Polarizer of Attitudes. *Journal of Personality and Social Psychology*, 12(2): 125.
4. Baked, D.F. 2010. Enhancing Group Decision Making: An Exercise to Reduce Shared Information Bias. *Journal of Management Education*, 34: 249–279; Greitemeyer, T. and Schulz-Hardt, S. 2003. Preference-Consistent Evaluation of Information in the Hidden Profile Paradigm: Beyond Group-Level Explanations for the Dominance of Shared Information in Group Decisions. *Journal of Personality and Social Psychology*, 84: 322–339.
5. www.reuters.com/article/2013/05/30/us-usa-volcker-easing-idUSBRE94S14620130530.
6. www.jimrogers.com/content/stories/articles/For_Whom_the_Closing_Bell_Tolls.html.
7. http://en.wikiquote.org/wiki/Jean_de_La_Fontaine.
8. Beber, A. and Pagano, M. 2013. Short-Selling Bans around the World: Evidence from the 2007–09 Crisis. *Journal of Finance*, 68(1): 343–381.
9. Zhu, N. 2016. *China's Guaranteed Bubble*. New York: McGraw-Hill.

14
HOW TO REFORM

Many of these decisions that are made by individuals, corporations, or governments may be viewed as investments—of wealth, capital, or political capital—in the hope of securing a better and more rewarding future.

So what lessons may all of these investors learn from this book?

Retail investors

The first lesson that any retail investor should learn from this book is that retail investors, on average, under-perform the market. This is primarily due to their own behavioral biases, especially over-confidence in their own investment ability, and lack of access to accurate information.

Second, retail investors have a strong tendency to chase trends and use recent market movements to predict long-term market fluctuations. This "representativeness bias" not only leads investors to make simplistic investment decisions but also hinders their performance by persuading them to invest in the market just as it is about to peak.

Finally, these behavioral biases are particularly pronounced among less sophisticated investors with limited financial literacy. Retail investors typically underestimate risk and market volatility and their impact on long-term investment growth. This limited understanding of risk lies at the heart of their over-confidence and simplistic investment decisions.

Avoid conspiracy theories

Many retail investors fall under the influence of conspiracy theories and use them as excuses for their own disappointing investment performance. Similarly, such theories may cause potential investors to steer clear of investing altogether. On the other hand, some conspiracy theories may reinforce active investors' attribution biases, which cause them to attribute profits to their own good judgment, and losses to forces that lie beyond their control. Those who succumb to this bias lack the motivation to learn more about finance and investment, and put little effort into improving their investment skills.

So, what should retail investors do instead?

Focus on long-term investment returns

There is no need to gamble on making extravagant, short-term profits. A safe and steady investment strategy will still generate substantial profits as long as the investor is prepared to wait a little longer. For instance, if one were to invest in stocks that generated annual returns of 8 percent, an original investment of 100 dollars would eventually mature into 1,006 dollars over the course of 30 years. Annual returns of 6 percent would generate 574 dollars over the same time period.

However, investors must take risk into account, in addition to returns. Given two alternative strategies that both promise to generate annual returns of 8 percent, an investor should always opt for the less volatile strategy, as this is likely to generate higher long-term returns.

So, even if a retail investor is unable to improve her annual returns, she should always look for ways to reduce the riskiness of her investment. We explore several of these below.

Diversify

Students in most introductory finance courses learn that diversification is one of the most effective means to achieve better investment performance. While the investment oracle Warren Buffett claims that his investment strategy is to put all his eggs in one basket and then watch over that basket like a hawk, most retail investors do not have the time or the inclination to do that. Instead, they are well advised to put their eggs into different asset classes, different regions, different currencies, and different products if they want to achieve steady returns and peace of mind.[1] Most Chinese households have not followed this advice—almost all of their money is invested in RMB-denominated assets—which is part of the reason why they are so nervous whenever the country's housing and A-shares markets start to fluctuate.[2]

In addition, it is worth mentioning that time is another important aspect of diversification. Very few investors possess the skill (or the luck) to enter and/or exit a market at the "perfect" moment. For example, many Chinese investors entered the Chinese A-shares market just before it peaked in 2007 and 2015, and some have yet to recoup the losses they sustained a decade ago. As we have seen throughout this book, this is a consequence of a particularly common behavioral bias that causes investors to jump into a rising market for fear of missing the boat. Given that this bias is so difficult to overcome, most investors are well advised to adopt a "dollar average" investment strategy, which involves investing roughly the same amount of money in a class of assets at regular intervals over a set period of time. This not only provides insurance against poor decisions prompted by behavioral bias but often obliges retail investors to behave like "value" investors, who invest more when the market is low and less when the market is high.

Consider transaction costs and net investment returns

Retail investors often neglect to take transaction costs into account when calculating their returns. Many of them do not even seem to care that such costs and management fees erode their returns. But the lower the transaction costs and management fees, the higher an investor's net returns will be, all else being equal. Consequently, transaction costs and management fees can be just as important as gross returns in dictating how much an investor actually gains (or loses) at the end of an investment cycle. Given how difficult it is to generate positive gross returns, retail investors should always pay close attention to their transaction costs and management fees in order to boost their net returns.[3]

Corporations

Sustainable growth

All listed companies have to cater to shifts in investor sentiment and demand for stocks with different characteristics if they want to stimulate a short-term boost in corporate value. However, it is important to point out that the capital markets invariably learn from investors' mistakes and adapt their responses to corporate strategies over time. Consequently, extended and aggressive corporate catering may damage a company's credibility among investors and prove costly over the long term.

Therefore, corporations must try to strike the best balance between their long-term and short-term objectives. To some extent, this can be dictated by where in the world they are listed. For instance, the Wall Street model prioritizes short-term earnings growth, whereas the German and Japanese models tend to focus on companies' long-term core value and competitiveness.[4] The US model certainly encourages rapid rises in share prices, and allows corporate executives to award themselves hefty bonuses on the back of them. However, the flip side of this model is that those executives may chase short-term performance at the expense of everything else, including ethical and even legal standards. In this sense, corporations need to realize that their short-term corporate financial decisions can have long-term negative impacts on the company's image and attractiveness to investors.[5]

Many listed Chinese companies have benefited considerably from the exponential growth in the Chinese real estate sector; indeed, many of them now enjoy greater revenues from real estate development than from their principal line of business. However, they should remember that real estate, like every other asset class, has its own cycles and risks. So, increasing a company's exposure to real estate fluctuations and neglecting the main line of business may jeopardize not only the firm's competitiveness but its very survival when the real estate cycle starts to turn.

Furthermore, while every company must care about its shareholders, it should also pay attention to a broader base of stakeholders, including bond holders, customers, employees, and local community residents. Cultivating healthy relationships with all these groups is essential if a company is to create a supportive environment that will support sustainable growth.[6]

Socially responsible growth

After 30 years of spectacular economic growth, Chinese corporations now need to pay more attention to nature, their local communities, and their stakeholders. Environmental degradation has increased at an alarming rate in China over those three decades, so the country's corporations must start to focus on maintaining the quality and sustainability of their raw materials and products, attend to the physiological and psychological health of their employees, and improve the communities in which they are based. Providing greater employment opportunities for their local communities, educating and training future employees, and building supplementary infrastructure will not only help companies establish harmonious relationships with those communities but also ensure their own long-term success.

Finally, Chinese corporations should increase their philanthropic activities and give more back to their communities. Of course this will provide assistance to under-privileged groups, but it will also help companies promote their visions and core values, and it might even generate valuable business ideas.[7]

Market regulators

Development of the Chinese bond market

The recent sharp rise in house prices in many Chinese cities and the subsequent changes to curb policies not only drew attention to China's attempts to transform its economic growth model but led to calls for further reform and relaxation of the Chinese financial sector. Indeed, the issue of financial sector reform has been central to many of the debates about China's economy over the past few years. To name just a few, small- and medium-sized companies' access to financing, local government financing and trust investment plans, the skyrocketing real estate prices, and excessive volatility in the equity markets have all been linked to financial sector reform. Indeed, many domestic and international experts agree that reform of this sector may hold the key to more comprehensive economic reform in China in the future.

However, there is no doubt that this is a daunting task. The market-determined interest rate, the internationalization of the yuan (to allow for usage and clearing of the Chinese currency overseas), and the opening up of flow under the capital account are three areas that are often cited when the issue of financial reform is raised. Reform of any one of these, let alone all three, will be a highly complex, lengthy process. At the same time, the deregulation of some financial markets, the launch of new financial products, improving investor protection and corporate governance, and making it easier for Chinese nationals to invest in overseas markets have also become important items on the reform agenda.

Thus far, however, policy makers, academics, and practitioners have failed to reach a consensus on a general timetable for reform, despite extensive discussions. They finally seem to have reached the conclusion that, as long as concrete progress is made in a consistent and orderly way, the focus should be on reforming and developing a small number of areas in the hope that this will stimulate progress in the others over time. Personally, I feel that we should concentrate on the development of a thriving bond market, as this seems a feasible early objective.

The development of a more mature and liquid treasury bond market is important because this market sets the benchmark rate and credit worthiness for all other fixed income markets in China. However, at present, the Chinese bond market's issuance and trading volumes are modest when compared to those in other developed economies. The secondary market is also relatively illiquid in contrast to the situation in the Chinese A-shares equity market. Although the National Association of Financial Market Institutional Investors (NAFMII) market fills some of the gaps in the secondary treasury market, more work has to be done to encourage trading and more realistic pricing in Chinese treasury bonds. Evidence from around the world suggests that the introduction of treasury futures and option contracts on treasury bonds will help with the formation of a market-determined interest rate. Moreover, if rumors were to spread about the introduction of treasury futures, this would go some way to solving the Chinese bond market's current liquidity problem.

The development of the treasury market will lead to improved liquidity, pricing stability, and an expanded investor base within the bond market. All of this should then pave the way to a more developed and integrated corporate bond market. At the moment, various segments of this market are regulated by the People's Bank of China (PBOC), the National Development and Reform Commission (NDRC), and the China Securities Regulatory Commission (CSRC). The existence of these separate regulation regimes causes unnecessary market segmentation, which in turn generates information disclosure asymmetry and regulatory arbitrage. Moreover, it results in low liquidity in each of the three secondary markets, which dampens interest in issuance in the respective primary bond market.

It is worth noting that only those companies with impeccable credit ratings can participate in the corporate bond market at present. Yet, one important function of every bond market is to evaluate credit worthiness. Consequently, companies with different levels of credit worthiness must be allowed to participate in the market if investors are to have an opportunity to evaluate them and express their opinions about their credit worthiness. This would help Chinese companies understand the value of financial responsibility and sustainability, and would motivate listed companies to improve their corporate governance and investor relations. The recent launch of a high-yield bond market suggests that the CSRC is aware of and determined to tackle this problem.

At the same time, municipal government bonds, which are already widely used in local government financing, should help local governments resolve many of the challenges they are currently facing, such as declining revenues and mounting debts. Whenever a local government secures financing through a municipal government bond, it has to disclose its budgetary plans and other detailed information to investors. Such disclosures not only increase potential investors' confidence in the product but also ensure that the local government's fiscal decisions are closely monitored. Ultimately, in addition to solving local government's financing problems, the development of the municipal bond market should provide local governments with a viable alternative to selling their land to developers, which in turn would dampen house price inflation throughout China.

Several provincial governments in the coastal region have been granted permission to issue local government bonds over the past couple of years. However, in an echo of the situation in the corporate bond market, the municipal bond market will be an effective arbiter of local governments' fiscal soundness—and a motivation for them to improve their fiscal sustainability—only if local governments with lower levels of credit worthiness are allowed to do likewise. Therefore, even—or especially—local governments that are facing serious fiscal problems should be invited to join the municipal government bond market. Such a market may well solve the local governments' debt problems and could also help many other stakeholders in the financial sector to manage their level of risk.

In summary, the development of the bond market could be instrumental in helping China achieve a market-determined interest rate, which in turn should aid the relaxation of capital account flow and cross-border usage and clearing of the yuan. Once the yuan has become a truly international currency, capital should flow freely across China's borders and the country should gain full integration within the global financial system. Needless to say, easy access to the international capital markets and an enhanced ability to manage risk in a global context will prove hugely beneficial to those Chinese companies that are committed to expanding and growing in the global marketplace.

Furthermore, the development of the bond market may "inadvertently" solve several of the problems facing the Chinese A-shares equity market. As bonds become a more viable financing option, Chinese companies will no longer be pushed through the narrow "drawbridges" of initial public offerings (IPOs) and seasoned equity offerings (SEOs) for their equity financing. Also, once the bond market becomes an alternative financing vehicle, the pent-up demand for IPOs should ease, as will the over-pricing and excessive valuations that are such features of IPOs at present. With the pricing reverting back to sustainable levels in the primary market, the secondary equity market will become more stable and attract long-term investing.

As more information is disclosed during bond issuance and transactions, companies engaging in these activities will face higher corporate governance expectations. Subsequently, if companies with listed equities fail to improve their own governance and investor protection, investors—especially retail investors, who face higher levels of information asymmetry—will probably vote with their feet and switch from the equities market to the bond market. Consequently, a thriving bond market may well force listed companies to curb their related-party transactions and tunneling deals, which have been undermining investor confidence in the Chinese A-shares market for several years.

Last, but certainly not least, a mature and well-developed bond market will offer a number of investment products to Chinese investors. As the Chinese population continues to age, Chinese investors, especially retail investors, will soon demand more investment channels and products with safer risk-to-return trade-offs. Once investors are able to obtain moderate, steady returns by investing in the bond market, they will start to invest less in the highly volatile A-shares market and the already prohibitively expensive real estate market. As a result, Chinese investors' more diverse portfolios will start to generate more wealth for Chinese households.

In summary, the development of a mature bond market has the capacity to kill numerous birds with one stone. Therefore, in the grand scheme of Chinese financial reform, it demands the policy makers' close attention.

The path to financial reform

Be it through interest rate liberalization, internet financing, relaxation of the capital account, or the development of a modern bond market, any major headway that is made in financial reform will surely bring tremendous opportunities and wealth to China's residents, investors, enterprises, and financial institutions. Even better, once this process of wealth creation gets under way, financial reform will promote diversification and alleviate the risks that have accumulated in the Chinese economic growth model. Therefore, the country's leaders have a duty to put financial reform at the top of the political agenda.

As it is, at present, many commentators are asking the same question: why is the pace of financial reform so slow?

Of course, as with almost every reform initiative in China, there are myriad differing views regarding both the direction and the pace of financial reform, even though most people share a similar goal. As any reform process is inextricably linked to people's current feelings as well as their expectations of the future, a better understanding of human nature and behavioral decision making may provide some fresh insights into why the next stage of financial reform may face significant reservations or even resistance.

First, people are inherently averse to change, as numerous psychological studies have shown. For instance, when participants in experiments are asked to evaluate objects in their possession and objects in other people's possession, they routinely over-value their own possessions and under-value the others' possessions, even when the objects in question are identical. One direct consequence of this is that people are often slow to initiate change, because they have a very strong psychological attachment to their present state. This helps explain why most reform initiatives face resistance.

Meanwhile, other psychological studies have helped us understand why the creation of new markets and new opportunities often serves as an easier path to reform. In experiments, participants may be assigned one of two simple objects at random, such as a candy bar or a mug of water. Then they are all given the option of exchanging their object for the alternative. In general, those with the candy bars feel that these are more valuable than the mugs, while those with the mugs feel that these are more valuable than the candy bars, so very few participants decide to exchange. However, if the subjects are asked to choose between two quite complex items, such as a personal computer and a mobile phone, they have to take a multitude of factors into account. This promotes more careful consideration of the pros and cons of each item, with the result that far more participants choose to exchange their item for the alternative. One implication of this is that it may be easier to initiate wholesale reform in several areas at once, as people are more likely to accept a complex reform package than a series of simple, minor reforms.

Other psychological studies have found that people are highly likely to make predictions about long-term development on the basis of short-term experience. As we saw in Chapter 6, people who have recently watched basketball games (with higher scores) tend to over-estimate random questions (such as the number of nations in Africa) than people who have recently watched baseball games (with lower scores). Similarly, experimental subjects who watch a video of people walking slowly subsequently walk at a slower pace themselves. Consciously or not, we are all influenced by our recent experiences. Consequently, we tend to become complacent about economic policies that coincide with prolonged periods of high-speed economic growth. Especially after the global financial crisis—during which most of the Western world's developed economies suffered serious reversals while China remained relatively stable and healthy—many Chinese investors and regulators argued that the country's financial system was already superior to all of the Western models, so there was no need for reform. China is now starting to pay the price for that complacency.

Finally, as we have seen throughout this book, people are universally over-confident when it comes to making subjective judgments about their own appearance, popularity, IQ, and so on: they over-estimate themselves while under-estimating others. For example, most retail investors feel that they have a talent for investment and are sure to make money from active trading. Unfortunately, statistical analysis of many large samples of investors reveals that most of them actually lose money; and the more they trade, the more they lose. To a large extent, this poor performance is due to over-confidence about the reliability of the information they receive as well as their own ability.

It is worth mentioning again that such over-confidence is not limited to individuals or retail investors—senior corporate executives and government officials also succumb to it, and sometimes to an even greater extent than retail investors. Consequently, policy makers may over-estimate their ability to manage the economy and stubbornly refuse to change tack, even when reform becomes essential.

We have reached that moment now. China's economic prosperity and social development rest on wholesale financial reform, so we all have a duty to encourage and initiate behavioral, legal, and institutional change. While every reform process carries a degree of risk, delaying any longer may be the greatest risk of all.

Overseas diversification

Data show that Chinese overseas direct investment (ODI)—investments made by Chinese companies in foreign countries—has increased considerably in recent years, and it seems inevitable that it will eventually surpass foreign direct investment (FDI) in China.

Since the global financial crisis, aided by quantitative easing and robust economic recovery, many emerging markets have increased their overseas investments, unable to resist the lure of profiting from businesses and projects in developed nations. Some of these investment opportunities are not only potentially lucrative but also strategically important for businesses that wish to expand from their home markets into the developed world. At the same time, as the currencies of some emerging economies and related assets continue to appreciate, many companies from those nations are looking for new investment channels for the considerable gains they have made from their domestic markets. International diversification and acquisition have thus become important factors in the equilibration of the global economy.

Chinese companies have concluded many blockbuster deals around the globe in recent years. Investments in Africa—many of which are related to infrastructure and natural resources—reflect Chinese companies' long-term global plans, beyond their immediate need for raw materials. In addition, faced with increasing domestic labor costs, many Chinese companies have moved their operations to neighboring Asian countries, where such costs are lower. Furthermore, Chinese real estate developers have snapped up prime properties and development opportunities in the US and Canada, which has heightened hostility towards the seemingly relentless overseas investment and expansion of Chinese enterprises.

However, it is in Europe where Chinese companies have been most active. The EU is China's largest trading partner, so it should come as no surprise that Europe has witnessed considerable investment from Chinese companies. Given the continent's geographical proximity and the historically close ties in terms of trade and investment, many Chinese companies have found investment in Europe complements their domestic business perfectly. Indeed, some so-called "China-themed investments" are specifically designed to help Chinese companies develop and ultimately penetrate the Chinese domestic market with the benefit of a European edge. For example, as Chinese consumers become more enamored with European luxury brands and the European lifestyle, many European companies are substantially increasing their market share in China. Although ever more Chinese companies are climbing up the design and manufacturing ladder, many of them have found it difficult to establish internationally renowned brands. Hence, to distinguish themselves from the domestic competition and gain international recognition, many Chinese businesses are investing in sectors and other companies that are in prime positions to profit from China's increasing wealth.

Of course, at the same time, many other Chinese companies are seeking to enter and/or expand within the huge European market. Such investments are important elements in long-term development strategies that aim to secure strategic partners, improve research and development capacity, patents, and technological know-how, and increase distribution channels. The timing could not be better for many of these Chinese companies as many European economies are still recovering from the European sovereign debt crisis and the global financial crisis, so they are desperate for capital and investment from outside the eurozone. As their fiscal situations gradually improve, many of these European countries are inviting outside investment not only in the private sector but also to help with the rebuilding or upgrading of their infrastructure, much of which dates back to the 1940s and 1950s. Unsurprisingly, Chinese companies often win the contracts for such projects, given the experience they have gained in infrastructure investment and construction over the past three decades. Indeed, many of these projects are not only funded but also managed and implemented by Chinese companies. This is certainly one area in which Chinese companies have turned their domestic expertise into global competitiveness.

Inevitably, China's economy has become more international as it has continued to grow, and individual Chinese companies are now engaging in more international investment than ever before. Local businesses across the globe are keeping a close eye on this international expansion and investment, some with enthusiasm and some with concern. Regardless of the vested interests of different parties, however, it is important to note that Chinese economic growth provides a wealth of opportunities not only for Chinese citizens but also for those of many other countries. After all, Chinese overseas investment is a necessary and healthy rebalancing of the persistent trade and capital flow imbalances that have been plaguing the global economic and monetary system over the past decade.

Last, but certainly not least, the recent tapering of quantitative easing in the US may finally herald the end of several years of unprecedented growth in emerging markets and China. There are already signs of capital flight out of a number of emerging economies. If this trend continues, these countries' ODI may soon outstrip the FDI they are able—or wish—to attract.

In summary

I truly hope that this book will help investors realize that it is not conspirators, not government agencies or regulators, not central bankers, not listed companies or mutual fund companies, but their own behavioral biases that are the greatest obstacles on the road to successful investment. All investors must learn how to increase their understanding of themselves, their investment objectives, finance, and risk if they wish to maximize their returns and minimize their losses.

Notes

1 www.theglobeandmail.com/globe-investor/investor-community/trading-shots/youre-not-warren-buffett-so-dont-invest-like-him/article5530869/.
2 http://corporate.morningstar.com/ib/documents/Brochures/2012_AdvisorCommunications Materials_Brochure.pdf.
3 Barber, B.M., Odean, T. 2000. Trading is Hazardous to Your Wealth: The Common Stock Investment Performance of Individual Investors. *Journal of Finance*, 55(2): 773–806.
4 Coffee, J.C. 2005. A Theory of Corporate Scandals: Why the USA and Europe Differ. *Oxford Review of Economic Policy*, 21(2): 198–211.
5 http://online.wsj.com/article/SB10001424127887324077704578358530334162430.html.
6 http://dealbook.nytimes.com/2012/05/14/group-calls-on-companies-to-focus-on-long-term-goals/.
7 Carroll, A.B. 1991. The Pyramid of Corporate Social Responsibility: Toward the Moral Management of Organizational Stakeholders. *Business Horizons*, 34(4): 39–48; McGuire, J.B., Sundgren, A., and Schneeweis, T. 1988. Corporate Social Responsibility and Firm Financial Performance. *Academy of Management Journal*, 31(4): 854–872.

INDEX

'.com' suffix 36, 91

1/N heuristics in over-simplified diversification 29

'accumulators' 100
Ackerlof, George 10
acquisition costs 81
active learning 77
Africa, investments in 12
age, and investment risk 21
Amaranth Advisor 1
American Online (AOL) 7
Apple 87
Apple Computers 33
Apple Electronics 9
aQuantitative 8
arbitrage 90
Argentine investors 29
Ariely, Dan 61
asset price theory, human behavior and 50
AT&T 8, 26
Autonomy 8

baby Bell companies 26
'balance sheet recession' 70
Bank of England 67
Barber, Brad 15, 16
Baruch, Bernard 69
Beber, Alessandro 105
behavioral biases: of governments and regulators 102–11; and investment decision making 28, 55–63, 80

brains, traders' response to risk vs. schizophrenics' 54
Bridgewater 65
Broadcast.com 7–8, 82
bubbles, reasons for: excessive liquidity 73; government support 73–4; investor irrationality and lack of sophistication 73; technological and financial innovations 72–3
Buffett, Warren 18, 24, 34, 43, 65, 104, 113
Burj Khalifa Tower, Dubai 71
buy-and-hold performance 3

California Public Employees Retirement Services (CALPERS) 7
Cantor Fitzgerald (CF) 94
CAO 101
cash as a benchmark 5
casino games 18
Cass Business School 105
Center for Studies in Economics and Finance 105
Chanos, Jim 104
Chen Jiulin 99–100
China: A-shares market 14, 43, 113, 117, 118; bond market, development of 115–18; bubbles generated by government policy 106–9; 'curb policies' 106 ; financial reform 118–20; foreign direct investment (FDI) in 120; formal banking sector 109–10; housing market 33, 106, 113; initial public

offerings (IPOs) in 88–9, 105–6; investment companies custodian fee 39; investors' excessive trading 13, 14, 15; market regulators 115–20; mutual fund investors, turnover rate 39; mutual fund management fees 39–40; overconfidence 14–15; overseas direct investment (ODI) 120; retail investors transaction fees 5; retail investors turnover ratios 13; shadow banking problem 109–11; skyscrapers 71; 'Spring Festival' effect 33; stock market bubble (2007) 42; trading turnover and online trading 16–18; under-diversified portfolio 23, 29–30; under-performance of retail investors 2; warrant bubble 68–9
China Asset Management Company Nikkei 225 30
China Audit Authority 110
China Aviation Oil (CAO) 83, 99–101
China Credit Trust Company 109, 110
China Railway Construction Company (CRCC) 101
China Securities Regulatory Commission (CSRC) 88–9, 90, 105–6, 117
China Southern Fund S&P 500 LOF 30
'China-themed investments' 120
Chinese Banking Regulatory Committee (CBRC) 110
Chrysler Building, New York 71
CITIC 100
CITIC Pacific 83, 100, 101
COFCO 84–5
COFCO TunHe 84
collateralized debt obligations (CDOs) 73, 110
collective decision making 102, 103
company name/ticker complexity 36–7
conspiracy theories 112–13
corporate acquisition, losses from 7–8
corporations, reform of 114–15
credit card industry 98
credit default swaps (CDSs) 66, 72, 97
Cuban, Mark 7, 8, 82
'cutting meat' 19

Dalio, Ray 65
Dallas Mavericks 7
Debt financing 89
decision making: government 102–11; investment, human behavior and 51–3
disposition effect 18–20, 24, 59

diversification, benefits of 28, 113–14
dividend payout, variations in 89–90
domestic stock, favouring 29; capital control as reason for 29–30
dotcom crash 103
Dutch house prices, central Amsterdam 70
Dutch stock market, nineteenth century 15

'efficient market hypothesis' 45
Empire State Building, New York 71
Enron pension fund 26
EntreMed 35
European sovereign debt crisis (2010) 98, 121
European Union 120
exchange-traded funds 57
Exxon 25

familiarity, stock selection and: geographical proximity 27, 36; sector 26; under-diversification and 24–6
fast thinking 47
'fat tail' nature of risks 97
fear 99
Fidelity 43
First Data 7
foreign direct investment (FDI) in China 120
framework thinking 99
FTSE global index 30
Fukushima tsunami 94, 97

'gamblers' fallacy' 41
gambling 56
Gates, Bill 80
gender and investment performance 15–16
General Electric 25
geographical proximity, stock picking and 27, 36
Global Crossing 26
global financial crisis (2007–2008) 1, 7, 66, 71, 73, 97, 98, 104, 105, 107, 121
Great Depression 71
greed 99
Greenspan, Alan 103
Gross, Bill ('Bond King') 98
'guaranteed bubble' phenomenon 108–9
GuoTai NASDAQ 100 30

'Halloween effect' in US investment market 32–3

hedge funds 90
herding and delayed reaction 34–5
Hewlett-Packard 8
high-risk stocks (high beta stocks) 6
holding periods 14, 18–19
HuaRui FengDian 88

ICBC 109, 110
illusion of control 18, 58, 99; barriers to entering the Chinese equities market 105–6; barriers to Chinese housing market 106
index funds 57
industry affiliation 36
information, stock-related, investors' responses to 35
information networks 27
information overload 77
informational advantage as rational reason for trading 20, 21
initial public offerings (IPOs) 86–7, 117; in China 88–9, 105–6
international diversification 29–30
internet bubble (1998–2000) 7, 8, 33, 36, 72, 90, 91, 98, 104
'internet finance' platforms 107
Investment Company Institute (ICI) 24
investment decision making, human behavior and 51–3
'invisible hand' principle 84

Jiangxi Saiwei 111
Jinmao Building, Shanghai 71
Jobs, Steve 111

Kahneman, Daniel 33, 41, 47, 50, 58, 59, 60, 61
Keiller, Garrison 52
Kerviel, Jérôme 1
Keynes, John Maynard 10
Kmart 26
Kohlberg Kravis Roberts & Co. (KKR) 7

La Fontaine, Jean de 104
'Lake Wobegon effect' 52
law of large numbers 78
Lawrence, Andrew 71
learning by investing 75–8
Legg Mason fund 40
Lehman Brothers bankruptcy (2008) 32
liquidity, as rational reason for trading 20, 21

local government financing vehicles (LGFV) 108
'long tail' nature of risks 97
Long-Term Capital Management (LTCM) 1–2, 6, 98
long-term investment returns 113
loss aversion 6, 18, 19, 20, 59, 99
lunar phase, influence on investor behavior 63
Lycos 8
Lynch, Peter 43, 104

magnetic fields, influence on investor behavior 63
magnetic resonance imaging (MRI), behavior and 53–4
management fees 114
MCI (Mass Mutual Corporate Investors Fund) 14
MCI Corporation (Ticker MCIC) 14
MCIC (MCI Corporation) 14
memories, limitations of 78
mergers and acquisitions (M&As) 7
Microsoft 8, 87
Military leaders, over-confidence of 103
Miller, William 40–1, 44
misguided stock picking 35–6
mistimed timing of stock picking 32–7
mood 99; decision making and 62–3
Morgan Stanley 1
Morimoto 2
MSCI global equity index 30
Munger, Charles 65
municipal government bonds 117
mutual fund fees 46
mutual fund investment: behavioral biases in 41–2; disappointing 39–46; excessive trading in 39; fixation on past performance 41; name changes 91–2; performance 57
mutual fund returns, driving forces behind: luck 44–5; risk 42–3; skill 44–5; style 43–4
mutual funds 4, 5, 23, 90; opening and closing mutual funds 92; with recent manager turnover 20

NAFMII 116
naive linear projection 41
name changes, mutual fund 91–2
neo-classical finance theory 19, 36, 53, 62
neuron tracking, behavior and 53–4

Odean, Terrance 13, 15, 16
oil crisis (1970s) 71
online trading and investment performance 16–18
opportunity costs of investments 76
ostrich effect 19, 76
overconfidence 14–15, 55–8, 99; behavioral bias 24; central bankers and financial market regulators 103; in Chinese housing market 33; in driving skills 18, 51–5; easy monetary policy 103–4
over-confident CEOs 80–5
overseas diversification 120–1

Pagano, Marco 105
passive learning 77
passive mutual fund investment 45
Paulson, John 6–7, 104
Pavlov, Ivan 75
pension funds 7; United States 25
performance of retail investors 3–6; long-term, comparison with market benchmark 2–3
PetroChina 88
Petronas Building, Kuala Lumpur, Malaysia 71
Pfizer 25
PiTuPi 91
Plaza Accord 70
'portfolio insurance' strategy 72
portfolio rebalancing as rational motivation for trading 21
portfolio risk exposure, as rational reason to trade 21
price-to-income ratio 106
price-to-rent ratio 106
probability theory 78
Procter & Gamble 25
professional investors' losses 6–7

'random walk' 62
rational reasons to trade 20–1
real estate bubbles 69–70; failure to last 70; Florida (1920s) 69; Hainan, China's housing bubble 69; Japanese 70
reform 112–21
'regression towards the mean' 72
Reinhart, Carmen M. (and Kenneth S. Rogoff): *This Time is Different* 72
'representativeness bias' 33, 41, 61–2, 99, 104–5, 112

'representativeness heuristics' 662
risk: due to corporate culture 99–101; due to financial innovation 97–9; due to individual behavioral bias 99; induced by success 97; and uncertainty 96–7
risk and return correlation 6
risk aversion 59
'risk free' investment 95
risk management 94–101; origins of 94–5
RMB 9
'rule of 72' 96

Scandinavian investors under-diversified portfolio 23
Schama, Simon 66
Sears Tower, Chicago 71
seasonal time adjustment and investor behavior and asset prices 63
seasoned equity offering (SEO) 86, 117
self-attribution 77, 78, 99
'self-fulfilling' prophecy 72
September 11, 2011 94
Shanghai Duolun Industry 91
Shanghai Stock Exchange 27
Shanxi Zhenfu Energy Group 109
Sharpe, William 95
Sharpe ratio 95–6
Shenzhen Stock Exchange 27
Shiller, Robert 10, 50, 70
short selling 90; ban on 104–5
'skyscraper curse' 71
skyscraper effect 71
slow thinking 47
Smith, Vernon 50
social networks 27
socially responsible growth 115
Société Générale 1
solar activity, influence on investor behavior 63
Soros, George 6, 104
Southeast Asian financial crisis: (1997) 6, 32, 71, 98, 103, 104; (2007–2008) 2
Southwest Bell 25
State-Owned Asset Supervision and Administration Commission (SASAC) 84
state-owned enterprises (SOEs) 82–4, 108
Sterling collapse (early 1990s) 104
Stewart, Martha 80

Index

stock market crash (1987) 6, 32, 72, 98
stock splits 90–1
sustainable growth 114–15
synergy, benefits of 81

Taipei 101 71
Taiwan: familiarity and investors' portfolio choices 25; retail investors' trading losses 2; under-diversified portfolio 23
Taleb, Nissim: *Black Swan* 96
taxation: as rational reason for trading 20, 21; selling stock and 20
telephone trading 1–17
Terra 8
Texas Energy Corp 7
Texas Pacific Group (TPG) 7
thinking framework, decision making and 58–61
Time Warner 7
Trans World Airlines (TWA) 29
transaction costs 4, 5, 14, 39, 114
transportation, illusion of control and 18
trend chasing 33
trust products 107
tulip mania 65–6, 73
turnover ratio 13–14
Tversky, A. 59, 61

UK railway mania 67–8
uncertainty 96–7
under-diversified portfolios 23–30; due to time limitations 27; familiarity 24–6; limitations in diversification 28; nearby stocks and stocks within the same sector 26–7

under-performance, conspiracy theories and 8–10
Union Carbide pesticide plant, Bhopal, India 94
US Federal Reserve 2; Survey of Consumer Finance 23
US retail investors: excessive trading 13, 14, 15; transaction fees 5; turnover rate 13; under-diversified portfolio 23, 24–5; under-performance of 3
USA: overconfidence 14–15; savings and loans crisis (early 1990s) 98; trading turnover and online trading 16–18

volatility 96
Volcker, Paul 103

Wall Street Crash (1929) 10, 69, 73
Wall Street Journal 35
Wang Yawei 43
wealth management products (WMPs) 107
weather, influence on stock market performance 62–3
whistleblower, role of 104
Winfrey, Oprah 80
World Trade Center, New York: attack (2001) 32; construction 71

Yahoo 7, 8, 82

'zero sum' game, investment as 55, 56, 57
Zhenfu coal mine 111
Zhongyou Core Select Fund 42
Zuckerberg, Mark 80

Taylor & Francis eBooks

Helping you to choose the right eBooks for your Library

Add Routledge titles to your library's digital collection today. Taylor and Francis ebooks contains over 50,000 titles in the Humanities, Social Sciences, Behavioural Sciences, Built Environment and Law.

Choose from a range of subject packages or create your own!

Benefits for you
- Free MARC records
- COUNTER-compliant usage statistics
- Flexible purchase and pricing options
- All titles DRM-free.

Benefits for your user
- Off-site, anytime access via Athens or referring URL
- Print or copy pages or chapters
- Full content search
- Bookmark, highlight and annotate text
- Access to thousands of pages of quality research at the click of a button.

REQUEST YOUR FREE INSTITUTIONAL TRIAL TODAY

Free Trials Available
We offer free trials to qualifying academic, corporate and government customers.

eCollections – Choose from over 30 subject eCollections, including:

Archaeology	Language Learning
Architecture	Law
Asian Studies	Literature
Business & Management	Media & Communication
Classical Studies	Middle East Studies
Construction	Music
Creative & Media Arts	Philosophy
Criminology & Criminal Justice	Planning
Economics	Politics
Education	Psychology & Mental Health
Energy	Religion
Engineering	Security
English Language & Linguistics	Social Work
Environment & Sustainability	Sociology
Geography	Sport
Health Studies	Theatre & Performance
History	Tourism, Hospitality & Events

For more information, pricing enquiries or to order a free trial, please contact your local sales team: www.tandfebooks.com/page/sales

Routledge
Taylor & Francis Group

The home of Routledge books

www.tandfebooks.com